WEEPING WITH JESUS

WEEPING WITH JESUS
The Journey from Grief to Hope

Ronda Chervin

ENROUTE

En Route Books & Media
5705 Rhodes Avenue, St. Louis, MO 63109
Contact us at contactus@enroutebooksandmedia.com
Find En Route online at www.enroutebooksandmedia.com

© En Route Books & Media, 2016

LCCN: 2016943947

Cover design by:
TJ Burdick
Back cover image credit:
C, Lauren, A Single Tear via flikr CC:
https://flic.kr/p/6VDi41

Paperback ISBN: 978-1-950108-34-3
E-book ISBN: 978-1-63337-103-3

Printed in the United States of America

Table of Contents

If you weep alone, you may drown in grief.
If you do not weep, you may become hard.
So weep with Jesus and find comfort and hope!

Introduction

1987-1994. Within this period of seven years, my mother died, my son committed suicide, and I lost my father, my husband, and my god-parents. Happily, there remained my twin daughters, also grieving, their spouses, and numerous grandchildren. In my own life, these events encompassed my fiftieth through fifty-seventh birthdays.

The greatest anguish came with the death of our son. Born when my husband was fifty-four and our twin-daughters were eight years old, with three miscarriages in between, Charlie's very existence seemed like a miracle. If love is measured by affectionate attention, no child could have been more loved. After his death, I would learn from psychotherapists that few suicidal teenagers were sufferers from neglect or abuse.

Charlie was nineteen when, in a state of depression, he cast himself off a bridge toward the Pacific Ocean. It seemed that the tears of my husband and myself would never cease.

Each death is as different as the relationship on earth that is lost. Some deaths, especially those that come after long illness, bring release. After some deaths there is a strong sense of the helping presence of the one who passed on to another life. What joy this brings! Some deaths bring acute pain; others dull and grey misery.

Expressions of grief also vary greatly from culture to culture. In many societies death is followed by loud public wailing, sometimes over a long and specified period of time. In others, tears after the first few weeks are a cause of embarrassment to others. But even if the pain is inward, it is surely grief. Some prefer to avoid the word "death" and substitute "passed away," "went home," or "went to the Lord." An amusing way of talking about a dead person I found in an old Irish practice is this: "he (she) got away from us!"

Over the years, emotions concerning loss undergo subtle shifts. For example, in the case of a spouse where there has been as much storm as peace, for a certain amount of time the death of one could bring fresh energy to the one left behind. After a time, though, along with the welcome absence of the bad, there could come a grey sense of all that is missing of the good that spouse brought to the relationship. The pain of loss in the case of such uneasy marriages, instead of being acute, could be a depressed sense of being shook up and insecure.

Feelings after a death could combine pathos and humor. For instance, a few months after my husband's death I kept a dental appointment. Always an ordeal for such a pain intolerant person as I am, I was brought almost to tears by the touch of the dentist's hand on my face as he injected the local anesthetic! Many people had hugged me since I became a widow, but none had touched my face as a husband would do.

From my own experience of bereavement and observation of others in pain over death, I came to the conclusion I placed on the first page of *Weeping with Jesus: the Journey from Grief to Hope*. If we weep alone, we may drown in grief. If we repress grief, we can become hard of heart. But if we weep with Jesus then we can receive comfort and hope. Over a period of time we can better understand why, after the Fall, God permitted death. Hiding in the wounded heart of Jesus, we will come to accept the death of loved ones as something that weans us from this world, making us more ardently desire eternal life. We will understand that Jesus truly is what He said he was: "the way, and the truth, and the life." (John 14:6)

My sub-title, "the journey from grief to hope," does not mean that grief from the death of a dearly beloved person ever entirely ends. Rather, with the help of God's grace, the gradual increase of hope for reunion in eternity makes the grief more bearable.

Of course, since my season of losses, I have met grievers with quite different kinds of losses: still-born babies, sudden death syndrome, accidental death of children, unexpected "early" deaths of siblings, grief for the aborted (go to Rachel's Vineyard www.rachelsvineyard.org). There is no way I can describe the deaths I did not experience myself with the same accuracy and breadth of detail as those that were mine. I believe, though, that the insights into grieving that came from the deaths in my own life will be meaningful to you even if the one that causes you the most misery is not in prominence.

In the past the word grief was used only to describe the sorrow of loss through death. Nowadays, pain coming from other kinds of losses such as rejection and divorce are also seen to involve grieving. Even though *Weeping with Jesus* is not designed to help with such forms of grief, what you read could help you encounter the personal love of Jesus for you in any kind of heartbreak.

Working on *Weeping with Jesus* has made me even more aware than before of how much Jesus wishes to be our consoler and hope at these crises of the heart. If your grief is raw and overwhelming, perhaps it would help you to read a few sayings right now that I have found the most helpful:

"You will never feel better until you know in your heart that your loved one is with Jesus in a better place."

"Would you prefer that the one who died had never lived so you would be spared this grief?"

"Would you rather be so cold that you would not have to grieve?"

"No one ever came to Christ unless his heart was broken."

"You cannot escape the anguish of loss, but with Jesus' love, you can survive it."

"Never picture those who died alone and floating in space – always picture them with the arms of Jesus around them."

At the end of each chapter I will include questions for personal reflection or group sharing. This will help you open yourself to the Holy Spirit to lead you on your journey.

My prayer as I close this introduction:

"Jesus, you who wept for Lazarus and at whose death Mother Mary shed the purest tears, may every griever receive comfort and hope from reading this book."

> "Blessed be the God and Father of our Lord Jesus Christ, the Father of mercies and the God of all comfort, who comforts us in all our affliction, so that we may be able to comfort those who are in any affliction, with the comfort with which we ourselves are comforted by God. For as we share abundantly in Christ's sufferings, so through Christ we share abundantly in comfort, too."
>
> (2 Corinthians 1:3)

For Personal Reflection and Group Sharing:

• Can you recall the first death that you knew about? What were the reactions of those around you? What were yours?

• Write down the names of those whose deaths you grieved.

• Were you able to meet Jesus in those times of grief?

• Are you grieving now? If so, write a prayer for hope.

The Pain of Loss

"Out of the depths I cry to Thee"

(Psalm 130:1)

"I am poured out like water, and all my bones are out of joint. My heart is like wax, it is melted within my breast."

(Psalm 22:14)

"A voice was heard in Ramah, wailing and loud lamentation, Rachel weeping for her children; she refused to be consoled, because they were no more."

(Matthew 2:18)

In this chapter we will view the pain of loss through the prism of accounts by different writers. Then we will reflect on the necessity of suffering bereavement. We will distinguish between good advice and suggestions that can be hurtful even if well meant. We will end with questions for your personal reflection or group sharing.

THE EXPERIENCE OF GRIEVING

Before we have experienced grieving ourselves, we might imagine that it is a phenomenon that takes place at the time of the death, at the funeral, and then for a short time afterwards. Not so. We don't say "I had grief today," but, "I am grieving," implying a long journey, sometimes lasting until one's own death!

In this chapter of *Weeping with Jesus* I have assembled descriptions of the pain of grieving, coming from past centuries to present day laments. The emphasis will be on the pain rather than hope. A Christian believer reaches out to Jesus in every circumstance in life, but in the case of grieving, at first the pain is in the forefront, not usually the consolations of faith.

But first, more about my feelings at the loss of my son. Pain at the loss of a child is usually pure, sharp and clear. Never have I felt such piercing all-encompassing grief. Before leaping to his death, my son sent us a letter of farewell, thinking it would arrive after the deed was done. We read the letter only to receive a phone call from him telling us he was on the way home from his retreat. Did he want to hear our voices one last time? I told him I would be flying from Los Angeles up to Monterey to help him drive home. My husband called the police. At the San Jose airport I called 911 to see if the police had rescued him. They told me they had no news. As it turned out they had found him half dead at the bottom of the bridge and were trying to save him. I guess they didn't want any interference from a hysterical mother. When I had almost arrived that foggy evening at the monastery where he had been making a retreat, I stopped at a pay phone. The police checked out my identity and then said "That one. He's dead," and then proceeded to ask me questions for their report.

After calling my husband, I began to wail. I was allowed to see my son before the autopsy the next morning. A miracle? Would Jesus raise him from the dead as He had Lazarus? No.

My husband was too prostrate with grief to come to Monterey. He decided to honor Charlie's desire to die at sea by having the body cremated with the ashes to be dispersed to the ocean. Later I learned that this practice is contrary to Catholic teaching. Cremation is allowed, but, if at all possible, the body or ashes should be buried in a Catholic cemetery where Masses are said every day for those interred. Meanwhile, my twin sister and brother-in-law had come down from Berkeley to help me.

At the monastery, I pulled my rosary out of my purse and started holding it all the time. "Pray for us sinners now, and at the hour of our death" became much more than a pleasant repetitious petition prayer. At my daily Mass I sat next to a replica of the Pieta feeling close to Mary who knew what it was to look upon a dead son's body.

For the first two months my husband and I would wake-up early in the morning and lie awake crying, holding hands and wishing we were dead also.

Then came numb resignation, and finally deep sadness punctuated with bouts of unbearable pain and tears. I thought my life should be over. How could I be a speaker and teacher if my wisdom couldn't save my son? Instead I became a witness of survival.

My husband died suddenly of cardiac arrest two years after the death of our son. There are marriages where the partners are so close that the pain of loss at the time of the death of one of them is as poignant as the loss of a child. My marriage was more complicated. Because as a teacher I am always grading students, I like to joke that our marriage went from A plus at the honeymoon stage, descending to C- by ten years after, and then ascended up to B+ by the time we were separated by his death.

My husband was 20 years older than myself. We always thought he probably would die first. Because he was a victim of chronic asthma with frequent seemingly fatal attacks, I was more prepared than many widows when death came. But it was a cardiac arrest, not a long drawn out lung disease that got him. I screamed as the paramedics tried to revive him and then manifested an old Jewish archetype by "rending my garment" – ripping my dress. Since an earthquake hit my area a few months afterwards there was little time for grief as the extended family we were living with needed to move with all the fuss and distraction that always entails. I think this was the main reason why pain of his loss was less immediate and more gradual.

One form my sense of loss took was unexpected. It was indecisiveness. Many widows report the same malady. Before Martin's death I thought of myself as extremely decisive to the point of obstinacy. My husband differed with me about some major values. I expressed my own opinions vociferously and championed my ideas about what we should do as a couple as if my opinions were absolutes. It was like a tug-of-war with me pulling frantically on my end.

After his death, without the counter-force of his resistance, I fell limp to the ground. Once more everything was totally up to me to decide, and I began to doubt. Did I really want to stay in this place or that? Should I leave this job for another? No husband to sort out the mess if I made a mistake.

In her book *Gently Grieving*, psychotherapist Constance M. Mucha writes about how the bereaved feel out of balance. "Nothing is the same after a loved one dies. Your world as you knew it moments ago is now changed. Your place in the family changes. Your sense of emotional and financial security is in disarray." (p. 13)

A related source of pain after my husband's death was the loss of the benefit of his virtues. Like many other married people, annoyance with my spouse's faults often outweighed gratitude for his good traits. Yes, my husband was more worldly, but he was also more savvy. When I lost $10,000 in a stupid car deal, I had to realize that Martin would never have made such a mistake.

Yes, my husband was more laid-back, but after his death I would have given a million dollars to see him relaxed in his recliner emanating jovial love of life and affection for our family.

In the passages to follow you will see how grieving has been experienced by people in different relationships. As you read, allow yourself to feel consoled by the knowledge that you are not the only one to suffer in ways that might seem extreme. In reading passages from the lives of the saints you may be surprised. I always imagined that they would be so trusting in the Lord they would have little grief. When I researched the lives of the saints with grieving in mind, I found that, for the most part, their hope in God did not take away grief, only purified it.

Here is a part of St. Augustine's famous account of the death of his childhood friend:

"...my friend fell gravely ill of a fever...he was baptized as he lay unconscious...I felt that our two souls had been as one, living in two bodies, and life to me was fearful because I did not want to live with only half a soul. ...I lived in a fever, convulsed with tears and sighs that allowed me neither rest nor peace of mind. My soul was a burden, bruised and bleeding....

"Neither the charm of the countryside nor the sweet scents of a garden could soothe it. It found no peace in song or laughter, none in the company of friends at table or in the pleasures of love (this was before Augustine's conversion), none even in books or poetry. Everything that was not what my friend had been was dull and distasteful. I had heart only for sighs and tears, for in them alone I found some shred of consolation.

"But if I tried to stem my tears, a heavy load of misery weighed me down. I knew, Lord, that I ought to offer it up to you, for you would heal it. But this I would not do, nor could I...especially as I did not think of you as anything real and substantial....(this was before his decisive conversion)

"...and if I tried to find a place to rest my burden, there was nothing there to uphold it. It only fell and weighed me down once more, so that I was still my own unhappy prisoner, unable to live in such a state yet powerless to escape from it. Where could my heart find refuge from itself?

"Where could I go, yet leave myself behind? Was there any place where I should not be a prey to myself? None. But I left my native town. For my eyes were less tempted to look for my friend in a place where they had not grown used to seeing him."

(Later, after his own turning his life over to Christ, he is able to understand that grief in a new light.)

"....the grief I felt for the loss of my friend had struck so easily into my inmost hearts simply because I had poured out my soul upon him, like water upon sand, loving a man who was mortal as though he were never to die...Blessed are they who love their friends in you and their enemies for your sake. They alone will never lose those who are dear to them, for they love them in one who is never lost, in God."

(Confessions of St. Augustine (p. 75-81)

Another famous account of grieving comes from a discourse of St. Bernard's to his monks about the death of his brother, Gerard:

"Why should I dissemble what I feel?...the excess of my grief takes from me all liberty of spirit, and the blow which has fallen upon me has quenched all the light of my soul....Hitherto I have striven, I have been able to master myself, fearing lest the sentiments of nature should overpower those of faith....

"I wished to concentrate my sorrows within myself; and they became only more intense and acute. How...my sufferings must needs come forth and be seen by others...that they may have compassion on me, and may the more tenderly console me....It would have been better for me to die than to lose you.

"(Gerard)...thou hast found far greater consolations; thou dost enjoy the immortal presence of Jesus Christ and the company of angels; but what have I to fill the void which thou hast left?...."

(Ratisbonne, St. Bernard of Clairvaux, p. 41 ff.)

Later, St. Bernard, writing about the death of a friend, insisted that he did not lose him, only sent him before to our Lord. (Ratisbonne p. 426)

St. Jane of Chantal at the death of her great spiritual friend St. Francis de Sales wrote:

"(my heart) adored God in the profound silence of its terrible anguish. Truly, I have never felt such an intense grief nor has my spirit ever received so heavy a blow.

"My sorrow is greater than I could ever express and it seems as though everything served to increase my weariness... The only thing that is left to console me is to know that it is my God that has done this, or at least, has permitted this blow to fall. Alas. My heart is too weak to support this heavy burden, how it needs strength.

"...it has pleased (God) to take from us that great flame that lit up this miserable world and let it shine in his kingdom...I am certainly too insignificant to merit...the contentment I had in seeing my soul held in the hands of such a great man who was truly a man of God."

(Francis de Sales and Jane de Chantal, *Letters*, p. 74)

St. Elizabeth Seton tells us about another type of grief in her writings after the death of one of her beloved daughters:

"It would be too selfish in us to have wished her inexpressible suffer-

ings prolonged and her secure bliss deferred for our longer possession...
though in her I have lost the little friend of my heart." (Chervin, *Quotable
Saints*, p. 150)

Venerable Cornelia Connelly lost a little son two and a half years old
in a tragic accident:

> "John Henry was the darling of the family, adventurous,
> light-hearted, and gay....He had run into the garden in the keen
> morning air with a huge Newfoundland dog. They had played
> together and somehow, between the large good-natured clum-
> siness of the dog and the young, inexpert limbs of the child, he
> had climbed up and fallen, or been pushed, into a boiler which
> was used outside the house for converting the raw maple juice
> into sugar. He took a long time to die. For forty-three hours,
> scalded and in agony, he lay in his mother's arms....Three
> words record the night....'Sacrifice! Sacrifice! Sacrifice!' "
>
> (*The Case of Cornelia Connelly*, p. 37-38)

Venerable Conchita (Concepcion Cabrera de Armida) of Mexico
tells us this about the death of her husband:

> "...this sword pierced my soul, without any assuagement, with-
> out any consolation. This very night, the Lord presented to me
> the chalice and made me drink of it drop by drop to the dregs....
> Oh! If I had not been sustained by Him, then through my great
> weakness, I would have succumbed....
>
> "What a model husband! What a model father! What
> an upright man! What finesse, what delicacy in his relations
> with me, so respectful in all his actions, so Christian in all his
> thoughts, so honest, so perfect in everything he did!"
>
> (*Conchita: A Mother's Spiritual Diary*, p. 49-51)

Of particular help to many is the experience of C.S. Lewis with the death of his wife, recounted in his book *A Grief Observed*, and made into the film *Shadowlands*. Joy, an American living in England, was married first in a civil ceremony to Lewis only as a ruse to allow her to remain in the country.

Joy was then only his good friend. During a seemingly terminal bout with cancer, Lewis discovered how deep his love for her really was. They were married by an Anglican priest. Joy had a remission long enough for the love in their late marriage to blossom and deepen.

When his wife died despite all their ardent prayers, the famous Christian apologist went through a severe crisis of faith. As you read these citations from *A Grief Observed*, you may find they resonate with your own:

"No one ever told me that grief felt so like fear...the same fluttering in the stomach, the same restlessness, the yawning. I keep on swallowing. At other times it feels like being... concussed. There is a sort of invisible blanket between the world and me...I dread the moments when the house is empty..." (p. 7)

"(Grief feels) like suspense. Or like waiting; just hanging about waiting for something to happen. It gives life a permanently provisional feeling. It doesn't seem worth starting anything. I can't settle down. I yawn, I fidget, I smoke too much. Up 'til this I always had too little time. Now there is nothing but time. Almost pure time, empty successiveness." (p. 29)

"One flesh. Or, if you prefer, one ship. The starboard engine has gone. I, the port engine, must chug along somehow till we make harbour. Or rather, till the journey ends." (p. 29)

"...this apathy, this dead flatness....Does grief finally subside into boredom tinged by faint nausea?" (p. 30)

"(We are told) people get over these things....Then comes a sudden jab of red-hot memory and all this 'commonsense' vanishes like an ant in the mouth of a furnace." (p. 7-8)

"No one ever told me about the laziness of grief. Except at my job – where the machine seems to run on much as usual – I loathe the slightest effort...It's easy to see why the lonely become untidy; finally, dirty and disgusting." (p. 8-9)

He writes about feeling that he was embarrassing everyone he met who doesn't know what to say and also being avoided by those who don't know what to say, "Perhaps the bereaved ought to be isolated in special settlements like lepers." (p. 12-13)

When no longer connected to his wife as her lover, his body felt "like an empty house." (p. 13)

He observes that even if there may be some new form of communication with the dead person, it doesn't come immediately and constantly, so the pain of separation is inevitable. (p. 15)

To remember her voice turned him into "a whimpering child." (p. 16)

"How pitiable to say 'She will live forever in my memory!' Live? That's is exactly what she won't do. It was (she) I loved. Not my memory of her." (p. 19)

In a fascinating analysis Lewis explains that memory is selective. "What we want is the real person who can contradict our fantasies about them....Kind people have said to me 'She is with God.' But what I am mourning for is her earthly reality with me." (p. 22) "We don't get over the pain," Lewis writes, "any more than a man whose leg is amputated is over it when he has a wooden leg to get about on. He will hardly ever forget it." (p. 43)

In our chapter about doubt and depression, we will read more from C.S. Lewis, but lest you think God left Lewis in this bitter state of mind, after much honest description of his grieving he reported that eventually "My heart (became) lighter...For one thing, I suppose I am recovering physically from a good deal of mere exhaustion." (p. 37)

And then he got some mysterious instantaneous sense of her – not an encounter but an impression. He realizes that he is remembering her better because he is grieving a bit less. He wanted to salute her and laugh somehow together. But then the pain came back with all the misery. It recurs. It doesn't stay put. "Sorrow is not a state but a process." (p. 46)

Finally, Lewis began to want to praise God for his wife and see her as a gift (pp. 46-49). He was able to see that what he loved in her was the image of God, and got the grace to believe, in the words of Blessed Julian of Norwich, that "all shall be well, and all shall be well, and all manner of thing shall be well." (p. 51)

Here is a fictional account of another man's grief after the death of his wife, whom he had tended in a long illness. (Anne Tyler, *Digging to America*, p.107)

"He thought, Why, this is just unbearable. He thought, I should have been allowed to practice on somebody less important first. I don't know how to do this. He forgot that he had practiced, on four grandparents and two parents. But there was no comparison, really. He had tended her illness for so long that it had become second nature, and now he couldn't believe that she could manage without him. Was she comfortable where she was? Did she have everything she needed? He couldn't stand to think she might be feeling abandoned....He kept her voice on the answering machine because erasing it seemed an act of violence. (A daughter calls just to hear her dead mother's voice again and again.)"

From the woman's side of losing a spouse I offer you this description by Sue Norris:

"To be bereaved (as a widow) is to die without dying; it is to lose everything you have known up to that point, but to continue as though it were not in fact all passed; it is to find that life has stopped but you have to continue walking seemingly legless; it is to love your children and friends still, and yet to have no heart, no feeling; it is to hear sounds and yet have no understanding of their meaning....I'm not myself, but who then am I?.... Somehow I knew that I just had to live day by day – not to push myself into anything but to live gently – quite a change from the energetic person I had been! But it was right, and somehow a new peace entered me, along with the sorrow.

(Sue Norris, *Holding Hands with God*, edited by Ronda Chervin, pp. 55-56)

Another woman, Leigh Mazaleski, wrote this poem about trying to comfort her mother at the time of the death of her brother, her mother's eldest son:

"No longer my mother she became a helpless child
Weeping as she lay across my bed
I stumbled through the first few hours
moving everyone through the reality we loathed to face feeling
frantic but with nowhere to go
needing to move, and so I paced she lost her first precious child
the risk taker who always knew he could win the one who never
stopped needing her love
And she buried him never to hold him again."

(*When Words Have Wings*, p. 62)

In the same volume, Mazaleski writes this about the look of the grieving:

"They move through the motions with bewildered eyes that tell the tale of death. Eyes weakened by tears, made expressionless by disbelief. They speak though their words are held captive by shock. They move though their bodies seem stiff and frail.... They have ...the kind of grief that lingers long after everyone else has returned to life. Now the struggling family must begin to crawl back to life from the deepest grave of sadness. They must find a new life as all was changed, in the blink of an eye. And in this dark moment, they have little energy to begin anew. They will yearn for the comfort of familiar surroundings while facing a different horizon." (p. 53)

Under the title "A Hidden Loss: Miscarriage," a mother, Katherine O'Brien-Johnston (*Holding Hands*, p. 73ff), writes about the grief of miscarriage:

"A child, a second-child, had been given to me, a child that I hoped to see and hold in just a few more months...Thanksgiving morning...the first sign of trouble appeared. At first I felt like I had a stomach ache, but then I began to feel like I was in labor... (the doctor thought the pain was a cyst but by Christmas it was clear she had miscarried)....How is a mother ever consoled for the loss of her child?...Miscarriage is a hidden loss – there is no body, no funeral, and many people think the baby isn't 'real' until born. They act and speak as though there had never been a baby...(years after) we still speak of her – and we still cry...the aching hole in our hearts longs to be filled. God has not given us another child yet. We wait, we hope, and we pray."

I had six miscarriages, and I want to add to O'Brien-Johnston's account that there is pain also for the siblings who have looked forward to that baby.

When my daughters told me years later about their grief over the miscarriages, I remembered a beautiful phrase I heard about newcomers to the family. A mother of twelve children used to announce a new conception to the already born, to help with sibling rivalry, she would say "Soon there is another baby coming to our family to love you."

Here are words about the accidental death of a son in a car accident by his mother, Shirley Schalk:

"No, no, no, not my Mike...the call came at around ten PM, January 12, 1992 – a car accident, and he wasn't expected to live the night. Dear God keep him alive till I get there. I screamed, I yelled, I cried...how could I wait till morning? There were no planes from Florida to Michigan till morning. Oh God, oh God, not Mike.... (when she got to the hospital the next day) my son was so swollen, tiny nose, slits for eyes. He was unrecognizable...I watched my son shake uncontrollably with no explanation from the doctors as to why....I prayed. The Lord said a war was going on for Mike's soul...During the rosary, I told Mike "Don't be afraid, let go and let God finish the plan for your life, whether it is to take you home with him or keep you here with us...He lived one week in a coma. (When he died) life went out of me. I miss him very much. (I believed he said yes to Jesus) but still there was a deep, deep agony of separation." (*Holding Hands* p. 98 ff)

And should grief for the death of a best friend have no place here? The poem "Funeral Blues" by W. H. Auden puts the pain of loss in less exalted terms:

Stop all the clocks, cut Off the telephone,
Prevent the dog from Barking with a juicy Bone,
Silence the pianos and
With muffled drum
Bring out the coffin,
Let the mourners come.

Let aeroplanes circle
Moaning overhead
Scribbling on the sky
The message He is Dead

. . . . .

He was my North, my South, my East and West,
My working week and my Sunday rest,
My noon, my midnight, my Talk, my song;
I thought that love Would last forever: I Was wrong.
The stars are not wanted now; put out every one,
Pack up the moon and dismantle the sun,
Pour away the ocean and weep up the woods;For nothing now
can ever come to any good.

THE NECESSITY OF GRIEVING

So much for descriptions of the pain of loss. Grieving is real and even inevitable in some form in the case of real bonds of love. Nevertheless, in our culture, and deeply embedded in my own psyche, there is the idea that grieving should be as short as possible. What presumably counts most is getting on with one's life, one's work, one's other relationships. Psychologists of grieving tell us that trying for closure too soon is, paradoxically, an obstacle to recovery. Repressing grief, in an effort to be cheerful or attractive or productive quickly, can lead to anxiety, depression, and other negative states. When we don't weep enough we are in danger of becoming hard. Sometimes less open to love with its vulnerability to loss?

Being a workaholic personality, after each of the deaths that took place in that seven-year period, I prided myself on my resilience. I needed to slow down and process my feelings, but this journey was blocked by some idea that long grieving would be a maudlin clinging to the departed one; a giving in to self-pity. I needed to learn that grieving is a necessity for the truly loving.

In his book *Love is Stronger than Death*, the philosopher Peter Kreeft describes our usual reactions to death as a spectrum where we may see death as a stranger, enemy, friend, lover, and, eventually, a mother. We may, indeed, arrive at such hope in Jesus that we can see our own future death and also that of beloved persons, as a friend, a lover, or a mother. Usually, however, we simultaneously will know death to be a stranger and an enemy with such related forms of grief as bewilderment and a sense of defeat.

In order to understand why grieving will almost always accompany the loss of a loved one, it is important to come to grips with an opposite theory. According to some, if we were more holy, in the case of the death of a good person, we would rejoice that he or she is with the Lord, instead of grieving over our own loss. In this connection, there is a book written about the religious attitude toward death by the great Catholic philosopher, Dietrich Von Hildebrand, that helped me understand my own grieving and that of others better. The book is entitled *Jaws of Death: Gate of Heaven*.

Here are some passages from Von Hildebrand's study for you to reflect upon:

"The 'natural' aspect of death is horrible and makes life seem pointless, but unlimited life on earth would also be dreadful and hellish." (*Jaws of Death*, pp. 2-4)

(There is) "the misery of losing a beloved person because with such persons I experience life in its fullness." (p. 6)

"Communication is gone, I cannot gaze into her eyes...dreadful emptiness...desolation....and then the monotony of routine life!" (p.6)

"Even if we believe in immortality, death still leaves the separation and loneliness." (see p. 6)

Only faith in God and in Christian Revelation can help. The sting is removed but there is still the fearfulness and it is still true that death is a punishment and that we are afraid of the unknown. (p. 18)

"Death is a terrible break with life, not a transition." (p. 60)

In line with this analysis is the fact that with death comes the loss of the part of ourselves that came alive in the presence of that person.

While some features of our personalities are the same with everyone, there are other aspects that only emerge as a response to some particular characteristic of the one we love. One friend may be able to make us laugh as no one else can. A baby brings out a tender cooing silly person that rarely comes out with other adults. We feel stretched in our souls when we are with a holy mentor. This loss of a part of ourselves in death is often the greatest in the case of the spouse of a long, good marriage.

Comforters can tell us that God will surely send us others to replace those who have left us in death. Surely, we will be grateful for love from any new person at this time of crisis, but there is no such thing as replacement. I love my grandsons dearly, but they never will be substitutes for my son.

A holy mentor of mine, Charles Rich, wrote a lot about death. Converted to the Catholic faith from a Jewish background at age thirty-three, he was so ecstatic at the promises of eternal happiness that comes with faith in Jesus that he wanted to die right away. He lived until he was ninety-nine! For more about his life and writings see www.friendsofcharlesrich.com. Many of the meditations that this lay contemplative wrote every day of his life concerned death and heaven. You will find quite a number of excerpts from his unpublished writings in *Weeping with Jesus*. Here is one concerning the necessity of grief:

> "It is God's will that when we hear that someone has died we should feel the loss as keenly as we can, for does not St. Paul say we are members of one another...Hard is the heart of the man who is not compassionately affected by the sight of someone who has died. We are all in need of God's compassion

and kindness in the way that we are all subject to the same sad end…How can we help being affected by the sight of a fellow human being brought to nothing by death?"

(Charles Rich, *Give me your Heart: Preparing for Eternal Life* – see www.friendsofcharlesrich.com)

A counselor with Survivors of Suicide whom I saw after the death of my son, brought me to understand another reason for the pain: dependency. Generally, we think of children as being dependent on their parents for the basics of care as well as for loving affirmation. This is true. But, often the parent is dependent on the child in a different way. In our fantasies this person we gave birth to or reared and educated is going to be everything we cannot be. For the sports' fan, the son might be slated to be a baseball star; for the paramedic the daughter could be a famous surgeon. In our case, my husband, who was too poor as a child to take music lessons, wanted our son to be the musician he wished he could have been. I wanted the same boy to be like St. Francis of Assisi. The counselor helped me see that such expectations could weigh heavily on a child; even make him or her feel doomed to failure.

So, with the death of a beloved child, we can no longer depend on someone else to carry our goals to fruition. It is now up to us to be that "star" or "saint," and humbly to accept that God has a different plan for our lives than we anticipated.

This insight about dependency and loss is part of why most of us feel much less pain at the death of older parents than that of spouses or children. The elderly parent is usually dependent on us, not we on him or her.

BAD AND GOOD ADVICE

Out of compassion many relatives and friends will be eager to give us advice as we grieve. Some of these suggestions are really helpful. Some, even though well-meant make it more difficult. We can add guilt to sorrow if we think we are not grieving in the approved manner!

From my own experience I would generalize by saying that any advice that makes you feel worse or that squeezes you into a box that fits others but not yourself is bad advice for you. It is best warmly to thank the advice-giver saying that you will ponder what was offered, but then put it in a sort of mental "pending file." Perhaps, if not now, it will be relevant on your journey.

There is such a wide spectrum of ways people cope with death. The most extreme I ever heard about was Queen Victoria of England's response to the death of her beloved Prince Albert. Apparently she insisted that his room remain intact with evening clothes laid out for dinner and a place setting for him at the royal table. On the other extreme would be someone throwing out everything associated with the person who died.

Most of us are in between somewhere. An enemy of clutter and lover of simplicity, in each of the deaths I went through I wanted to get rid of most of the accumulated stuff, but save special precious objects as mementos. From my mother I saved a blue and white kimono she had worn at the birth of myself and my sister and kept for the rest of her life. I treasured photos of her pregnant and then with us wearing that kimono. Later when Charlie died I wrapped a lock of his hair, cut from his corpse, in a piece of my mother's kimono and stuck this strange looking object into my bra near my heart.

One of my daughters wrote about what her father's bathrobe meant to her before and then after his death:

"Whenever I felt sick or sad, I took my father's robe….The robe was soft and thick and far too warm. Sweat hides like an animal in its folds….It is no sooner put on then you begin to seek escape….For two years I periodically stole the robe. The robe was nothing less than the entire symbol of my father's love for me: not even thinking, in the dark and afraid, no time for delving into sub-consciousness, I fled to the robe at every crisis, knowing I must have it in the wordless way a baby reach for a favorite toy to replace Mama's arms in the night. When my father died, I couldn't bear to sort through his possessions for a long time. Each object carried a weapon aimed straight at the hole I struggled to fill: the mortal wound of my grief, unscabbed again. The robe, however, I wore….It hangs on the hook in my closet, and I wear it when I feel sick or sad."

(*The Fabric of Our Lives*, ed. Ronda Chervin, p. 141-143)

My father made the process of remembrances for those he would leave behind simpler. A few years before he died he insisted that all guests tell him which things they wanted. These he labeled with their names on the back so his executor could give them to us right away. Happily there were no conflicts.

I believe that the person who was chosen as the executor of the dead person's will has a right to decide about minor items. I wouldn't have wanted to hear well-wishers telling me that I should save piles of things not valuable to anyone in the family as a sign of love. On the opposite side, I am sure Queen Victoria didn't want to hear any hints that her grieving was excessive in her mode of expression.

"Bad advice" can also come from insufficient consideration of the character of the bereaved person with respect to the contemplative/active polarity. A very thoughtful inward person may desire long periods of quiet prayer after the death of a loved one. A more extrovert person may need to be as busy as before, even though eventually he or she will need to pray in depth.

Those like me who do well with group processing will benefit from grieving programs in the parish or elsewhere. Others could not bear to speak out their feelings even to family no less than to strangers. Suggestions can be offered, but bereaved people don't need pressure.

Nowadays it is common at funerals for the family to plan the occasion, often with special touches. Among the most unusual I have heard about is the showing of a film made by a man a few months before his death. In the video he speaks to those who will attend the funeral, expressing his deepest wisdom and singing a holy song. Since he was a Hollywood actor, this came out as a beautifully constructed personal statement moving and inspiring to family and friends.

In our family there are poets, artists and a sacred dancer: my sister. At our family funerals the artistic ones make collages of photos taken from the beloved person's life. Poems composed for the occasion are read and we are invited to a ritualistic dance.

Others might find all such displays to be theatrical and even sacrilegious! They don't need to hear advice on how to do it up. They need to have the quiet simple funeral of their choice, emphasizing the need for prayers for the soul of the deceased. That also will give the sorrowing the greatest peace.

We need to ponder carefully what is good to say and what sometimes hurts others inadvertently. For example, a friend told me that when her mother died when she was still a child, her father told her that "God took her." This led her to an abiding fear of God who could snatch anyone away at any time. It would have been better to say "Probably we will live long lives, and one day you'll see your Mom in heaven."

As to good advice, I will pass on to you some that helped me.

Talk not only about the trauma of the death, but about the good times in your life with a person who died.

Before birthdays of the deceased and other family holidays, work out a strategy. Expect to feel depressed as birthdays and holidays loom on the horizon. Christmas without him or her – unbearable! Quite a few friends have confirmed my experience on this: the horrible feelings precede the occasion. At the time of the actual celebration there is some joy even if it is less than when that loved one was part of it. The first few holidays I was unprepared for this prelude of more intense grief. Then I began to expect it and prepare more by making sure I was doing something that would help in the weeks before or on the day. I had a tape of my son Charlie's musical compositions, and I would choose a different friend each year to listen with me as I wept for him. Of course this drew me closer to those friends willing to go through this ritual with me.

Having Masses said for the souls of the departed on the anniversary or as close as possible add the feeling that I am doing something for him or her of supernatural value.

Because grieving is so long a process, we cannot hope it will just get better quickly. A psychotherapist, Joseph Nicolosi, told us that the sorrow lessens in such tiny increments that it's hard to realize it is getting more bearable. Looking back I realize that with each important loss at first I would think of him or her every moment I was awake; then maybe fifty times a day, and then slowly less and less. Never gone is the sadness or tears, but slowly diminishing all the time piercing desperate grief of the onset.

When friends say, "I don't know what to say," realize that it is not words you are looking for but love. You are missing the felt, visible signs of love of the person who died. A hug or a kiss will usually mean more than "consoling" words.

Expect that in your pain you may make some mistakes trying to find compensatory love. Common examples are widows or widowers making a child into a pseudo-spouse with heavy unreasonable demands. We widows can also get ensnared by exploitative men and widowers by manipulative women. With attachments to good people, we can set ourselves up for wounding rejection if we try to make others meet needs of ours that do not fit in with their God-given characters or life-plans. If psychologically harmful or sinful patterns become repetitive and destructive there may be need for professional counseling, as well as sacramental confession, spiritual direction, and contemplative prayer.

As a widow I went through many years of turmoil with recourse to psychotherapy and heavy spiritual direction. Much healing came from such helping counselors and mentors. Still, I found myself trying one place after another in relation to my work as teacher and speaker. I thought of myself as a kind of pilgrim soul. Perhaps. But an even more telling image of myself, if more pathetic, was that I had become like an Indian Asian beggar going about with a bowl to fill with rice. The rice I sought was the missing love of my husband and son. As soon as my bowl was empty I would leave for another place hoping for more love. Presently I am living with a daughter, her husband, and five children. This seems like a more stable way to receive not only the perfect supernatural love of Jesus, but also the more earthy family love that was part of my vocation before those deaths.

There is much helpful advice on grieving from professionals.

In preparation of this part of my chapter on pain of loss, I went to the web to see what good advice I could cull from the work of Elisabeth Kubler-Ross (1926-2004). Ross was a Swiss born psychiatrist whose major work took place in the United States. Her book *On Death and Dying* published in 1969 became a best-seller. Even though I had lost interest in her when I heard that she was involved with New Age ideas and practices, I remembered that she had significant insights into the process of dying and of grief.

Here is a brief list of her suggestions for the grieving with my comments:

Attend support groups

I went to three different grief groups after the deaths of my son and husband. One was a simple parish group; another was supervised by a professional counselor; another was run by intern M.A. counseling students at a Catholic University. Each one provided needed help, especially to realize how many shared the same kinds of suffering.

Go to a trained mental health specialist

I found insight and new ways of coping with the challenges of the suicide of my son and, then, with my new state in life as a widow from three therapists. Two of these were not Christian believers, but they could be helpful because many of my problems had more to do with emotional log-jams than with moral issues or problems of spirituality. The last was a Seventh Day Adventist with an ecumenical outlook who combined standard psychological methods with healing prayer.

Journaling

Ross recommends this for those who like to write. Since I have done journal writing for many years, I can recommend it with conviction. (One of these journal books is published under the title *Becoming a Handmaid of the Lord* including notes from the time of the deaths in my family - see bibliography. Other journal books spanning later decades of my life can be obtained by visiting http://www.rondachervin.com) What I write in my journal is a record of impressions and thought in relation to prayer. It is helpful to have a record of special graces given, to read when dark times threaten to overwhelm one.

Eating Well and Resting

Grieving is draining physically as well as emotionally. I find that eating good nutritious regular meals vs. snacking aimlessly, and sleeping a lot, even if I have to take a mild sleeping pill, is necessary to avoid becoming sad and moody.

Exercise

Yes. This always helps even if it is only to clean the house vs. moping around.

Help from Faith Communities

Our Christian faith is all about hope and eternal life. What better time to immerse myself in Christ's mystical body, the Church, than when bereaved.

Create Rituals

It is very important to me to pray regularly for those who died in my family. There will be more about this in later chapters. I like to play favorite music of my husband and commune with him as we did together when he was here with me. Those who live near the graves of their beloved death find solace in visits.

Allow Emotions

All experts on grieving advise letting the tears flow. I find that this expression is not something I can force. They come suddenly and often unexpectedly because a memory is triggered by a present event. Over time I also have become grateful in new ways for how much my parents or god-parents gave me that I took for granted.

Earlier on I cited a book about grieving by a nurse-psychotherapist, Constance M. Mucha. (*Gently Grieving: Taking Care of Yourself and Telling Your Story*. New York: Paulist Press, 2006.) Here I will add suggestions she made in the book not covered by the parts of Kubler-Ross' advice already given:

"It is good to tell the story of the person who died over and over again about their life and their death." (p. 4)

You need to be gentle with yourself and with others. For instance, you may not be able to send thank you letters or make phone calls for awhile. Let a friend do it for you.

Balance tears with fond memories.

"Remember that children and teens often will blame themselves for deaths of parents or siblings. For instance, a six-year-old can think, 'I could have told my Dad the truck was coming.'" (p. 5) They need reassurance. In the case of death of a sibling they also need to be told over and over again that the parents don't wish they had died instead!

"In your grief take into account that when a sibling dies you lose part of the past, present and future." (p. 5)

"Expect to find things hard in ways you wouldn't anticipate such as replacing a husband's name with yours in the phone book or on stationary." (p.6) In the case of the death of a child expect to find it hard when strangers ask you how many children you have. Should you count the dead one in the list or go into explanations where you don't feel like awakening all that grief?

"Be careful not to attribute to grieving physical ills such as not being able to sleep well which could have quite other causes that need to be looked into." (p. 16)

"If you don't like eating alone eat many small meals." (p. 17)

"Be aware that the second year after a death may be harder than the first because more of the numbness is gone." (p. 29)

"Smiling can be good in spite of grief – like an underwater swimmer coming up for air. Also laughing, not at the loss but other funny things in life." (p. 43)

I believe that nothing helps so much as reaching out to Jesus for comfort and strength. Much more about this will be found in later chapters.

For Personal Reflection and Group Sharing

- Describe the pain you experienced when people close to you died.
- What helped you endure these miseries?
- List qualities of each beloved person who died. Then pray until you see how those qualities are also in Jesus and others you love.
- How have you experienced the Holy Spirit as your comforter: through Scripture, consolation in prayer, the love of others for you?

Doubt and Depression

"I moan like a dove. My eyes are weary with looking upward.
O Lord, I am oppressed; be thou my security."

(Isaiah 38:14)

Besides the pain of loss, many grievers also experience grave doubt
and/or dark depression. Some have conscious anger at others such as doctors judged to have been incompetent; relatives who failed to help in financial ways or with their time; God, who didn't seem to realize that they
could not endure such a loss. About anger I will try to provide help in the
next chapter "If only…" In this part of *Weeping with Jesus: The Journey
from Grief to Hope*, we will study successively doubt and depression.

DOUBT

Consistent materialists think that death is the end. They usually think
that there are no immaterial realities such as God, angels, or souls that
could continue to exist after the heart stops beating and the brain goes
dead. Ghosts are thought to be superstitions.

Others who are not strict materialists, and who are unsure of the soul, angels, or God, might think there is some sort of spiritual stuff that lives on and that can perhaps be contacted.

Strong believers in the reality of the immaterial or spiritual, including souls, angels, and God, ought not to doubt that the soul of a dead person could survive the end of bodily life. But even those who have strong belief in the after-life, at the time of the death of a loved one may find buried doubts surfacing. The issue of immortality can be abstract during everyday life. But when it is a question of the soul of one we love and possible reunion in an after-life, immortality becomes a most gutsy survival concern.

As an example of an extreme battle with doubt by a strong believer, we return to C.S. Lewis' reaction to the death of his wife. As you read Lewis' account of his desperation, you might want to star those that match your own doubts.

Trying to pray for his wife after her death, C.S. Lewis wrote,

"I have a ghastly sense of unreality, of speaking into a vacuum about a nonentity.... You never know how much you really believe anything until its truth or falsehood becomes a matter of life and death to you. It is easy to say you believe a rope to be strong and sound as long as you are merely using it to cord a box. But suppose you had to hang by that rope over a precipice. Wouldn't you then first discover how much you really trusted it?"

(*A Grief Observed*, p. 25)

Yet he realized that if he doubted whether his wife existed in some form after death, then she never existed as a person at all:

"I mistook a cloud of atoms for a person. Since she was a person not just a material entity she must still be." (p. 25)

Lewis' doubts were especially surprising to himself and to his readers because in his masterpiece *The Problem of Pain*, C. S. Lewis provided the world with one of the best explanations of why human suffering was compatible with a God of love. But then when he, himself, was in the deep pit of misery over the death of his wife, all his old arguments fell by the wayside.

Bitterly he doubted the God of love and wailed, "….where is God?...go to Him when your need is desperate, when all other help is vain, and what do you find? A door slammed in your face, and a sound of bolting and double bolting on the inside. After that, silence." (*A Grief Observed*, p. 9)

Later in the grieving process he saw that God is silent but not uncompassionate – He is real but He doesn't answer our questions directly. The real answer undercuts the questions (see p. 56). But such comforting experiences came only after much deeper doubt.

At one point Lewis played with the idea that God was a demon who hated him. (p. 10 and p. 26) He considered the possibility that when Jesus on the cross asked God why had He forsaken him, maybe He had been forsaken.

Could God be a cosmic sadist? (see p. 27)

Such dismal thoughts would be check-mated by more rational ones. A sadist God would never have made all the love and beauty in the world. Lewis asked himself:

"From the rational point of view, what new factor has (Joy's) death introduced into the problem of the universe? What grounds has it given me for doubting all that I believe?...I had warned myself not to reckon on worldly happiness. We were even promised sufferings." (p. 31)

His problems with doubt forced Lewis to realize that his previous belief was not that deep. But then he countered this unhappy self-revelation with an opposite thought: why should I think that more horrible thoughts after a death are truer than thoughts when I felt more sane? (see p. 33)

"You can't see anything properly while your eyes are blurred with tears." (p. 37)

In this connection a mentor once told me when I was grieving the death of my best friend, "Your leaning post has relocated, that's why he seems distant."

With time Lewis began to consider the death of his wife in other terms. Could it be that they had reached the apex of their love on earth and that God wanted to move them on to a more supernatural plane? (see p. 40) He even was able to consider that the death of his wife might be a cross sent to try him.

Finally he came to a decisive sense of her post-death reality. It was not a vision or a locution but a strong sense of her mind impinging on his, an intimacy that was solid but not sensory or emotional. (pp. 57-58)

Many years before the death of so many family and mentors, I wrote a book called *Victory Over Death*. It was not about grieving, but about how to face one's own death in the face of doubts and fears. This book is now out of print. I will include here some of the best insights from that book: ideas I still think came from the Holy Spirit.

Doubt about survival after death sometimes comes from a long series of disappointments leading to the feeling that maybe the promise of life everlasting is just another illusion. (*Victory Over Death*, p. 9)

These unhappy experiences could lead to the question: Why does everything betray me? The work into which I plunged all my youthful energy – how did it get so entangled in fussy details, petty problems, that it lost its thrill and became just a job to endure? How did my first love lose its glow? My children change from innocent flowers, young saplings, to resentful teenagers? How did my once strong body become this distasteful, painful burden? How is it that I who gave myself so totally to loved ones now find myself alone? … Might not the idea of heaven be the ultimate false promise, too good to be true?

And yet we do hope against hope. I believe that our ever-abiding yearning for happiness is itself a sign that even if all our earthly wishes have played us false, yet union with God and our loved ones is not a vain hope. Once I wrote this short meditative poem:

What is yearning made of?
a rubber-band stretched from time to eternity?
Not so compact as a wish, nor as straight as an arrow, yearning
spreads yet encompasses no object,
bursts through flesh yet is that flesh's cry.
Yearning, what are you made of?
are you echo of God's sigh?

In his famous poem, "The Hound of Heaven," Francis Thompson (1859-1907) shows us how it is only through having to let go of our illusions of human happiness that we can embrace the absolute source of love who has been waiting for us.

"I fled Him, down the nights and down the day;
I fled Him, down the arches of the years;
I fled Him down the labyrinthine ways
Of my own mind; and in the mist of tears
I hid from Him, and under running laughter.
Up vistaed hopes
I sped;
And shot, precipitated
Adown Titantic glooms of chasmed fears,
From those strong
Feet that followed, followed after.
But with unhurrying chase,
And unperturbed pace,
Deliberate speed, majestic instancy,
They beat – and a Voice beat More instant than the Feet –

41

"All things betray thee, who betrayest Me."....

Whom wilt thou find to love ignoble thee,

Save Me, save only Me?

All which I took from thee I did but take,

Not for thy harms,

But just that thou might'st seek it in My arms.

All which thy child's mistake

Fancies as lost, I have stored for thee at home:

Rise, clasp

My hand, come,"

Halts by me that footfall:

Is my gloom, after all,

Shade of His hand, outstretched caressingly?

"Ah, fondest blindest, weakest,

I am He Whom thou seekest!..."

(The Treasury of Catholic Wisdom, pp. 605-609)

Yes, we hope that our deepest yearnings will be fulfilled by God in eternity. Yet, surrounded by materialism we can half think that anything we can not see and touch cannot be real, including, of course, the so-called souls or others that are supposed to escape from the death of the body. At funeral Masses we are reminded of Jesus raising Lazarus from the dead and of His own resurrection. Our hearts take hope. But then in the dark of night in our bereavement, doubt can come back.

I find it helpful at such moments to recall what philosophers such as Plato, Augustine, and Thomas Aquinas, basing their conclusions on reason, teach us about the reality of the immaterial soul and its immortality.

Here is the way I like to summarize such perennial teachings about the soul and its survival:

Consider your essential self, the "me" that persisted from conception to the present. What is this self? I cannot be just the body, for biologists tell us that over a seven-year period every cell in our bodies has been replaced. Yet you are the same person. If not, how explain memory, culpability, praise? Do not say that the "you" of 2006 remembers a different "you" of 1990. You don't refuse to pay a traffic fine on the grounds that you are no longer the same person, or refuse an award because you are no longer the same you who did the praiseworthy deed.

But all such continuity of the self means that an immaterial (non-physical) self persists amidst change. The essential self could, in principle, continue to exist, even after the physical change we call death.

A further proof that we have a part of us that is not physical is that we cannot measure the soul. A saint doesn't have a five-pound soul and a sinner a one-pound soul. A thought in your mind is immaterial – a serious one "weighs" no more than a trivial one, a truth no more than a lie.

What cannot be measured because it has no parts, cannot fall apart as does the measurable physical part of us that comes to pieces. And the soul? By nature, what is not matter cannot be destroyed by matter.

That spirit is different from body and therefore capable of surviving death can also be shown by examining the soul's tenacity in the face of physical suffering. The following is excerpted from the book by Richard Wurmbrand, *Sermons in Solitary Confinement*. Wurmbrand was a 20th century atheistic Jew who became a Lutheran pastor. He was imprisoned by the Communists in his country of Romania and tortured in a solitary cell because he was so successful in converting even hardened communist jailers!

Here is what he wrote to his own soul:

"The body needs few things in order to be fully satisfied, simple food, warmth, exercise, rest, and a partner of the opposite sex. My body had all these things (before conversion) but, notwithstanding, I was not happy; I sighed for something more. Who was this "I," dissatisfied when the body had plenty of all that it needed. It was you, my soul.

"It was you who wished to know, out of purely scientific interest about galaxies far away, and about facts of prehistory which have absolutely no influence on my bodily state. It was you who took delight in art and philosophy...

"Don't you see, my soul, how right Jesus was in saying that 'man does not live by bread alone'? (Now in prison) I get one slice of bread every Tuesday. And what bread! But I do not just vegetate. I live. I sometimes laugh heartily at jokes which I tell myself, being alone in my cell....I lead a life of worship. All this is you. Say, my soul, 'I am.' You saw me dancing when I was in unspeakable pain. You saw me dancing with heavy chains around my ankles. Who was that one who exuberantly rejoiced? It was not my body. My body had no reason to dance...

"Take knowledge of yourself, my soul, and take knowledge of your incomparable value. The body will die. Around me prisoners are dying because of the great hunger, the cold, and the tortures, but who has ever seen a soul die? I have lost everything I had in the world, but if you are saved, I shall have kept the pearl of greatest price."

Wurmbrand's stunning argument links logic and experience. Others believe in the immortality of the soul based on heightened moments of seeing the beauty of the soul of a child in his or her eyes. Others are impressed by accounts by those who "died" and were resuscitated whose souls roamed around the hospital and later reported information they could not have known from their death beds.

I liked reading this slightly sarcastic passage from a letter by a 3rd century holy Father of the Church to a skeptical friend:

"When you have put off mortality and have put on incorruption, then you shall be worthy to see God. For God will raise up your flesh immortal with your soul; and then, having become immortal, you shall see the Immortal, if you will believe in Him now; and then you will realize that you have spoken against Him unjustly. But you do not believe that the dead will be raised. When it happens, then you will believe, whether you want to or not..."

St. Theophilus of Antioch, *The Faith of the Early Fathers*, Volume 1 (Collegeville, Minnesota:The Liturgical Press, 1970), p. 73-74)

"Yes, yes, yes," you may respond. "But, but, but, still with the pain of this suffering, I wonder. Why would God allow this much pain if He loves us?" Behind this doubt, I think there is an assumption that life on earth should be happy. We know that God could remove all suffering on earth. Jesus did heal people. But not always; more as a miraculous sign. Why not admit that, after the Fall, it is not God's purpose to eliminate suffering on earth. He brings good out of it. What He wants is more love of God and neighbor, not less suffering. But He did send Jesus to promise an eternity of happiness for those who put their faith in Him.

Here is a different way of putting it from the writings of an ardently Christian Russian writer, Dostoevsky, who was riddled with doubt for much of his life:

"My immortality is necessary if only because God will not be guilty of injustice and extinguish altogether the flame of love for Him once enkindled in my heart. And what is more precious than love? Love is higher than existence, love is the crown of existence, and how is it possible that existence should not be under its dominance?...if there is a God, then I am immortal."

(Dostoevsky, *The Possessed*, trans. Constance Garnet (NY: Macmillan, 1931), p. 623)

In another novel, Dostoevsky has a holy saint respond to a woman obsessed by doubt, that the only remedy is active love. Why is that? St. Thomas Aquinas taught that we can only love ourselves loving. When we show love to others, we see ourselves as lovable. Then it is easier to believe that an all-knowing God can love us, in spite of the sins we repent of. And if He loves us, of course, He wants us to live with him for all eternity. And if we loved the one who died so much, doesn't God love him or her a thousand times more?

Even if they were religious before, people imprisoned in the concentration camps during World War II would usually become afflicted with doubt. A holy Protestant Christian, Betsy Ten Boom, imprisoned because of hiding Jews, consoled those whose faith wavered with the truth, "If you know Jesus, you don't have to know why."

In the book already cited, *Jaws of Death: Gate of Heaven*, Von Hildebrand recommended that to increase our faith "we must turn away from the things surrounding us so as to concentrate on the absolute reality of God. When we become silent, when we let God speak, we can strengthen our faith." (p. 108)

"To the extent that faith is the axis of our life, a strong, alive, and deeply personal faith, the glorious aspect of death will triumph in us over the fearful and anxious aspect." (*Jaws of Death*, pp. 109-110)

Here is a related quotation from the early Church theologian, Tertullian:

"(Inordinate grief) bodes ill of our hope, makes a lie of our faith; and we wound Christ when we do not accept with equanimity the summoning of any by Him, as if he were to be pitied…If we grieve impatiently when others have obtained the desire of Christians, we show ourselves unwilling to obtain it."

The Faith of the Early Fathers, Volume 1
(Collegeville, Minnesota: The Liturgical Press, 1970) pp. 125-126)

DEPRESSION

The word "depression" will be used here not to mean a clinical state of chemical imbalance that could be modified by medicine, but rather a prolonged steady state of grim sadness.

Depression and doubt are often partners. If doubt leads finally to despair of hope, sadness and low feelings will be the usual outcome. Here is an account of the feelings of a father after his son's death in battle in Iraq.

The father was a democrat, not especially pro the Iraq war but proud of his son when he enlisted. He was reluctant to consider the Iraq war to have been a mistake because then his son's death would be meaningless. He had to hear the views of those who claimed that the soldiers were under-equipped because of the indifference or negligence of the Bush administration. The father wanted to escort his son's body back from Baghdad. Instead he got to see it at the nearest airport to him and could see his son's face once more. He rejected having a photo of his son at a Catholic peace vigil because he thought it was more politically motivated than a memorial. Someone said, "thank you for your sacrifice," which he didn't like because it had not been his choice. He wept often thinking "What's it worth? A democratic Iraq? I just want my son back." (See George Packer, *The Assassin's Gate – America in Iraq* (N.Y.: Farrar, Straus and Giroux, 2005) p. 374 ff.)

The author of the book about the Iraq war does not depict the father as a doubter of God because of his sorrows, but more as a bewildered, depressed person with no answer. It is interesting that the young man's mother, divorced from the father, had become a born-again Christian and thought that her son died to fight the forces of evil.

A widow writes: "Why is that bird still singing? My life had halted three hours earlier when my husband died suddenly…A fog and thousands of miles separated us.…How was it possible that the rest of the world continued?".… My life is buried there too, I thought, as I stood by my husband's grave after his funeral…the pains were not only from my loss but from all the unfinished business that it seemed would now not be finished. What could I do about all those things I wish I hadn't said, or that he had said and I hadn't understood?…how could we ever come to grips with all this pain? But no, here was my first lesson: "we" were not going to come to grips – "I" was." (Sue Norris from *Holding Hands with God*, p. 53 ff.)

In the case of loss of family members, if their death means living alone after years of daily companionship, depression can easily follow. Some grievers have relatives or friends stay with them while they consider a new life style. Often they will decide to move closer to living family members.

Sometimes depression after a death comes from unresolved guilt feelings. Did the conflicts in a relationship become so severe that his or her death was wished? The psychotherapist Dr. Constance M. Mucha, earlier cited, claims that those who spent a long time after a death helping others cope, may not have processed their own grief sufficiently, with the result a sense of depression. (p. 21)

I believe that the tradition in many cultures of wearing distinctive garb after the death of a close relative probably provided a definite period for mourning with a kind of closure when the garments were exchanged for other colors. The Kubler-Ross foundation sells black armbands for the grieving to wear for a time individually chosen.

In some countries old women grieving one death after another simply keep wearing black for the rest of their lives. Most of us would consider such a practice as a cause of depression, but I wonder. Is it less depressing, for instance, in a desperate desire to flee from the pain, to become an alcoholic?

After my husband's death I fell into what I called the grey night of the soul. St. John of the Cross believed that spiritual progress depended upon passing through the dark night of the soul. But my long night was not so much black as grey. I knew that God was with me, but I felt low and depressed for a long time.

I was advised to accept those feelings, but at the same time come against them. Not so much by direct confrontation, but by opening up time to let in more light to my battered heart. "Do what helps you," a friend advised. At first I thought this was a ridiculous idea. Of course we do what helps us. Then I realized I don't always do what helps me. I often flee into workaholism instead of spending time in the beauty of nature, music, and art. Beauty is a foretaste of eternity. When we experience it, we can sometimes get a sense of the beloved lost one immersed in this beauty, if not right away because of purgatory, moving toward it. A memorable instance of this truth came from an invitation to a concert. The woman who asked me to come with her was in my suicide survivor's group. Her teen daughter had killed herself around the same time my son had. Her adult son was in the orchestra. One of the pieces was Richard Strauss' "Death and Transfiguration." This was an old favorite I had not listened to for a long time. After tumultuous and poignantly sad parts there is a breakthrough into a luminous ecstatic sense of eternal bliss. When that part came, I grabbed the hand of my friend and both of us felt a sense of the presence of our beloved children, not with us in the auditorium, but there – in the beautiful beyond, redeemed by our Savior.

In the greyness that can come with grieving, moments of enjoyment of beauty are not luxuries but necessities. They make real for me these lines from St. Herman of Reichenau, "The whole of this present world has become mean and wearisome, and on the other hand the world to come has become so unspeakably desirable and dear that I hold all these passing things as light as thistledown. I am tired of living." (*Quotable Saints*, p. 47)

On quite a different note, a death can bring depressed feelings because it forces us to accept what philosophers call contingency: that life on this earth can be snuffed out at any moment. We humans cannot hold our bodily existence in a tight grip. Even though we know that an unending life on earth would be tediously unbearable, the idea that the life in this world may end in a second is frightening. The actual death of another can trigger off sadness about our own contingency. When we feel depressed about this, we need to hide in the heart of our Savior who is not contingent, but a perfect, unchanging being in order to feel consoled.

Let me close this part of the chapter with another quotation from the poet Leigh Mazeleski:

"Let the depth of their pain open their hearts so that they will learn the comfort of sharing with others. Let their new depth make them rich with emotion, so that one day they will have a passion for living. Let their depth of spirit endure, so that in their lifetimes they will find a joy they had never imagined, a faith they never expected, and a strength they never knew existed."

(*When Words Have Wings*, p. 53)

For Personal Reflection or Group Sharing

- Did you have doubts about God or the after-life at the time of the death of beloved persons?
- If you did have doubts, what truths or experiences brought you out of doubt?
- Think of moments when you were able almost to see the soul of someone who is now dead. Let yourself dwell in those moments and feel reassured that the soul is more than the body.
- If you are now in a state of doubt, write a prayer asking God to reassure you.
- Is your grief different from that of non-believers? If you have more hope, thank God for the gift of faith. Compose a prayer for those who are hopeless in the face of death.
- Do you give yourself enough time to "hold hands with God" in the dark or do you distract yourself to avoid depression and then feel sometimes even sadder between bouts of activity?
- When Jesus was forlorn and felt abandoned, he prayed, "into your

hands I commit my spirit" (Lk. 23:46) When we think of our beloved dead, we can pray, "into your hands, I commit his/her, their, spirits." Picture your loved one embraced in the arms of Jesus who is calling him or her by name.

- Praying the Stations of the Cross in Church can help you unite your sufferings with those of the Lord in His passion.

- In a group for grieving it was suggested that we write a letter of goodbye to the one who died. If you feel depressed, try writing one. If you like to draw you might include an artistic rendering of your feelings.

- A grief counselor who is a dancer suggests putting your pain into motion.

- Make a list of those parts of creation you consider to be the most beautiful. As you remember a time of being at the ocean, looking into a baby's face, etc., let God tell you how this will be in eternity when such experiences will be free from annoying accompaniments such as smog, traffic, bugs, dirt. Even if we must pass through purgatory on the way, we hope that one day we will all be together experiencing such beauty. Anticipate this in hopeful meditation.

- There is a famous mural from Forest Lawn Cemetery showing Jesus welcoming crowds of people into heaven. See if you can find that picture or some other from the tradition of Catholic art to remind you that life on earth is not our final destiny.

If Only...

I can't run away from this day
Although I fill each block of time
I can't push the sadness away
As the horror creeps into my mind
The questions return on this day
And acceptance of the unknown is slow
And it's the details of "the news" I replay
When it's his face that I long to see so
….A hint of fantasy lightens my day
And I imagine that it was all just a dream
That violent death took my brother away
Instead I ache of wounds unseen

(Mazaleski, *When Words Have Wings*, p. 63)

WITHOUT AN ANSWER

When we demand God's intervention then we close the
doors to hope and our sight becomes narrowly focused
When we ask for a miracle then we are bound for disappoint-

ment and we starve existing only on expectations

When we place blame in our sorrow then the root of our pain becomes lost and we waste precious energy on anger

When we bargain in desperation then we lay a plan for failure forgetting that our Father cries our tears

When we punish God for our loss then we place our souls in lonely torment discarding the only one who knows

When our acceptance is contingent upon answers then we become exhausted in endless search and our progress is chained to closure

(Mazaleski, *When Words Have Wings*, p. 58)

Most often when a loved one goes through a long dying process surrounded by relatives and friends, we have had lots of time to come to terms with the impending separation. There will still be grief, but there usually will be less issues of "if only...." such as in the case of sudden deaths in accidents, murder, or suicide.

- "If only I didn't turn my back to pick up the phone when my baby choked to death on that marble the older kids left on the floor?"
- "If only my daughter left the house 5 minutes later, she would still be alive!"
- "If only the police had caught that serial killer one day earlier!"
- "If only my parents had been more loving about my unwanted teen pregnancy, I would have kept the baby or given him or her for adoption."
- "If only I had shown more love, would my husband not have taken his own life?"
- "If only God had understood how much I needed to marry my fiancé, maybe he would not have let her get killed in that accident."

In the case of relationships with unresolved conflicts, there are other types of "if only" questions.

- "If only my wife had gone to 12 Step for her drinking, would we have become more happy together before her death?"
- "If only my father had said "I love you, my son," even once in my life, would I feel only sadness at his death, and not this bitterness?"

In the case of C. S. Lewis' extended ponderings about the death of his wife to cancer, the if only question came down to considering God a sadist for allowing her to die. Eventually he would write:

"Why do I make room in my mind for such filth and nonsense?... Aren't all these notes the senseless writhings of a man who won't accept the fact that there us nothing we can do with suffering except to suffer it?" (p. 29)

He began to realize that thinking of God as a cosmic sadist was a form of anger, a way of hitting back – telling God what he thought of him.

"Anger makes you feel better for a moment because it seems like retaliation." Eventually he realized that he might be to blame if he wanted her back even if it would not be good for her. (pp. 32-34)

The widow Sue Norris wrote that after the sudden death of her husband, "I came to real anger with God. Being a Christian is about becoming integrated, whole, and now through no fault of my own, being bereaved was to become at once split, disjointed, shattered, scattered...It just wasn't fair."

But then after awhile she came to realize that only God could remold her vulnerable self into something new. In her advice to other widows she says that it will not help to close oneself off through anger. "We are all such controllers, for all we may say our life is God's and mean it. When it comes to the crunch, we really don't like him interfering in these uninvited and dreadful ways ...melting...it's fiery." (Sue Norris from *Holding Hands with God*, pp. 54-57)

UNHELPFUL WAYS OF DWELLING ON THE "IF-ONLYS"

Feelings of anger at the death of a loved one through the carelessness of a drunk driver, the malice of a murderer, the mental confusion of suicide, or death before reconciliation are natural and to be expected. Though no sin is unforgivable, it is still a terrible thing to drive drunk risking the life of others. You could be very angry at the one who died if the accident was their own fault, as in driving on drugs. What grace of God it takes to forgive someone who murdered a person you love whether it be a stranger who killed, say, in the course of a theft, or a crime of passion, or an insane serial killer.

How angry one can be that someone threw away his or her own lives, possibly in a period of despair that could have been overcome?

What makes righteous anger bad is if it festers without an end, building to the desire for revenge. Instead of joining a crusade against drunk driving, with potential good results, what good fruit can come from nurturing hatred for the victimizer? Rightly it is said that hate hurts the angry one more than the target. (See Chervin, *Taming the Lion Within: Five Steps from Anger to Peace*)

I have heard of young adults angry at God or fate because their parents died too soon to be at their graduations or weddings. Again, the feeling of pain because of the absence of those whose death deprived us of their presence is not blameworthy, but a sign of the depths of the love they gave us while alive.

What becomes unhelpful is a dwelling on such a cross in the form of withholding trust in God's loving providence. Sometimes this anger manifests itself in envy of those who have what we lost. After the death of my son, I found it hard to visit friends with teen sons, especially if those sons were affectionate to their parents. Once I realized this explanation of the depressed feelings I had seeing young men hugging their mothers, I was able to expect my initial reaction and finally with time to rejoice that a friend still had sons on this earth who loved her so much.

Feeling guilt over a death is almost inevitable for family in the case of a suicide. With the help of the devil, it is easy to blame ourselves as if our behavior or omissions were the sole cause of the tragedy. For a year after my son's death I would go over his whole life up until then dismally adding to the list of my crimes: "if only I had gone on welfare when my husband became disabled, instead of working outside the home, maybe Charlie would have been more secure." This idea would be accompanied by replays of little Charlie at four years old standing numb with sadness inside the gate of the Montessori school I sent him to while I taught at the University.

About this particular guilty memory, it helped me to meet a mother of another teenage boy who had taken his life. She was a typical at-home Mom whose greatest joy was to be there constantly for her children. She was berating herself that because she was under-educated and at home she hadn't developed the sensitivity to understand her son's artistic personality!

It also helped with guilt to talk to an acquaintance, Joseph Nicolosi, a psychotherapist. He explained what is called the eternal child syndrome. Some young people can't stand to leave childhood behind to become adults. They may try to avoid adulthood through drugs, drink, extreme dependency, and sometimes suicide. When Dr. Nicolosi told us this, I said I wished I had sent Charlie to Nicolosi for therapy. His response surprised me:

"No. Most likely I could not have helped him. The eternal child is convinced that he understands his destiny better than anyone else. He or she usually rejects the counselor. Such eternal children also usually disdain all pills designed to deal with their depression, for such medications would quench their creativity. It is too demeaning for a free spirit to take pills."

This helped me with guilt about "if only" I had found the right counselor. Even if you can't find an expert to relieve this type of guilt, you will need to gradually accept the fact that God allowed you to be in circumstances that made it hard to find a solution that later seemed possible. For example, the adult children of an elderly person might discover after the death of a parent that there was a sure cure just 50 miles away at a research hospital.

"If only I had known!" Not guilty. Exactly. If you had known, you would have gotten your mother or father there even at great sacrifice. God, for His own reasons, allowed it that you didn't know.

After each of the major deaths in my family of my mother, father, son, and husband, I found comfort in going to sacramental confession:

"Father, I would like to make a general confession of everything I ever did that was unloving to ____. (I specified typical sins I committed against each one such as harsh judgment, non-forgiveness, nagging, anger, etc.)

This helped me to realize that, yes, I was at fault but that didn't mean I was responsible for their deaths. I also made general acts of forgiveness for the ways they hurt me.

Another bad way of dwelling on "if only" has to do with the imagination. I always tell the newly bereaved that they must avoid at all costs picturing the loved one alone, far away, floating in space. Shortly after the death of my son I woke from a nap and felt his soul very close, as if he were looking through the window. This short mystical vision left me full of happiness. He wasn't far; he was close.

This grace was accompanied by an intriguing insight. We think the dead are far away because it might be a long time before we see them again, face to face. But time is not space. The realm of purgatory or heaven is not far from us, just mostly invisible to us.

Now I advise those left behind to always "picture" the deceased as near even if invisible and untouchable. Best is to picture him or her in the arms of Jesus. We will see when we study Scripture and Tradition that even though purgatory is a place of purification, there is great joy because the souls there know that they are saved. So, we do not need to picture them in our minds as far away, alone, and probably in misery.

GOOD WAYS OF COPING WITH "IF ONLY."

Misery loves company is an old adage. Groups devoted to helping the grieving can help with "if only issues." They take us away from isolated brooding. In the case of Survivors of Suicide groups for families and friends of those who succeeded in taking their lives, reference is often made to the enigma of suicide. It is stressed that we will never be satisfied by any explanation given – it will always be an enigma. Why? Because none of the reasons that can be given force another person to make that tragic choice. Another person under the same conditions will decide to live on carrying those crosses.

I needed to listen carefully to how the Holy Spirit was talking to me through my religious friends. A priest told me, "God didn't call Charlie home, but he welcomed him home." Another friend suggested that maybe God sometimes lets those die who cannot carry the burden He called light.

We grieving people are in danger of drowning in our sufferings, asking about "why me?" or "if only." We need to grab on to the life-line of Catholic teaching. I found John Paul II's encyclical "On the Christian Meaning of Suffering" (1984) helpful, especially because he, himself, had suffered so much during World War II, from the Communist regime in Poland, when a terrorist tried to assassinate him, and then from his last illness.

Because in the past it was thought that all suicides go to hell, it helped me enormously to read what the Catechism teaches:

"We are stewards, not owners, of the life God has entrusted to us. It is not ours to dispose of....Grave psychological disturbances, anguish, or grave fear of hardship, suffering, or torture can diminish the responsibility of the one committing suicide. We should not despair of the eternal salvation of persons who have taken their own lives. By ways known to him alone, God can provide the opportunity for salutary repentance. The Church prays for persons who have taken their own lives."

Catechism of the Catholic Church (2280-83)

This knowledge made it possible for me to pray for him in this way:

"I beg you, Lord, to save my dear one who in desperation took his own life. I believe that you love him a thousand times more than I do. I believe that at the last moment you offered him your divine embrace. Please accept my prayers and sufferings now to join to your redemption of this soul. According to your wisdom, I beg you for a sign that my beloved one is saved."

Books about healing of memories by Linn and Linn also helped me with grieving miscarriages.

Many grieving over "if only" speculations are comforted by receiving what can be interpreted as signs from those who have gone before. The question of the legitimacy and validity of signs is a confusing area. It is not Catholic teaching that we can take personal visions or locutions to be infallible. But that does not mean that they are bogus and should always be dismissed as dangerous.

True, we are not allowed to insist on communication with the dead.

"All forms of divination are to be rejected...conjuring of the dead...recourse to mediums...all conceal a desire for power over time, history, and, in the last analysis, other human beings.... They contradict the honor, respect, and loving fear that we owe to God alone."

(*Catechism of the Catholic Church*, 2116)

On the other hand, Scripture is studded with instances of God-given signs. Prophets such as Elijah proved the existence of Jahweh in the face of the false prophets of Baal through the sign of a miraculous fire. (1 Kings 38)

Certainly, we should not demand that God send us a sign of the salvation of a beloved person who died. But we can certainly be grateful for a sign that is consoling. One of my tests for things seen visibly or interiorily or heard audibly or "in my heart," is whether the sign seems like the sort of thing I would imagine and concoct or whether, instead, it seems surprising and not inventible.

After my son died, I would have liked to have a vision of him being rescued by his guardian angel, to whom I had been praying for him just before his decision for suicide. I would have liked to have heard him tell me he was saved in spite of everything. I didn't get such signs. But surprising things did happen. For example, the grandfather clock in our living room, always wound up for 24 hours at 11 PM each night, stopped at 4 PM, the day and time Charlie jumped off the bridge. After I called Martin to announce the death, Martin heard Charlie tell him, "Dad, don't worry. I'm okay." These welcome words were not in the style of a supernatural pronouncement but more the way a teen might say it. My brother-in-law, not a Catholic familiar in any way with such a sign, smelled roses when none were around on the wintry coast of California. My sister audibly heard her nephew Charlie tell her, "I love my sisters. Father, forgive me and hold my hand. But Mother, you taught me not to fear death."

A month and a half after his death, I received this locution from Jesus: "I let him jump because I could not stand to watch him suffer so much. The purpose of life is to get a foretaste of heaven and to want eternity. That is what he wanted. He had his foretaste of eternity in the joys of life. He was weaned by his sufferings from wanting to live any more. You will find him in My heart." It certainly sounded more like Jesus than like me.

Charlie was a composer. At a concert given by his friends for the anniversary of his death, my daughter, Diana, saw a vision of Charlie smiling.

While writing this book I have had a strong sense of the real presence of what I could only call the personal flavor of both Charlie and Martin.

My sense about signs is that since we are meant to continue on in life without our beloved dead, it would be complicated if they felt really present all the time. We are not to drag them back to us, but more to let God stretch our souls to reach toward eternity.

After the death of Mike Sweeney, one of his disciples, the lay contemplative referred to earlier, Charles Rich, wrote,

"Mike appeared to me today, and he looked right at me, as if he was alive, and he is alive, existing in Him who is Life Itself... he seemed to want to say something to me which he felt I could not understand...showing there is a kind of wall separating the living from the dead which will exist until we will be with them in the state of glory...that the souls of the faithful departed exist in Christ is confirmed by these experiences of them that now and then come to us....something of the other world is made evident to us when we feel that someone who has left this world shows himself and herself to us...these experiences are shrouded in mystery...but it was vivid and real, making me feel it was the soul of Mike looking at me, and not just some kind of false vision and chimera... these are glimpses, tiny glimpses, seeing if we get the full flush of them we could not go on living, the joy and delight they bring with them, forcing the soul to take leave of its bodily habitation. For Mike Sweeney the battle is over, and he won the war, the war we still have to keep fighting. How lucky he is as are all those who already are safe with God."

Many years ago one of my best friends, Professor Frank Sullivan, of Loyola Marymount University in Los Angeles, was dying of a long, painful illness. We were all worried about how his wife could bear the inevitable separation. It certainly seemed like a sign from him when right after hearing of his death from the doctor at the hospital his wife found that their toilet seat had cracked in half!

Shirley Schalk, in *Holding Hands with God*, wrote this about the many signs that came to show her that her son who died in a car accident was saved in spite of his wayward life-style. "On Holy Thursday, after his death, I gazed at the heavens and…I saw my son standing in white…to the right of Jesus with many little children…From time to time, mostly at Mass, the Lord allows a brush of a kiss on my cheek….many of Michael's friends (some of whom were touched by Mike's death bed conversion) saw Mike in the light reassuring them. (p. 100-101)

In closing this chapter I would like to offer this prayer:

"Dear God, I accept the fact that I cannot undo anything in the past that might have contributed, however remotely, to the death of my loved one. Please keep me from compulsive guilt and self-flagellation. I place my dearly beloved one into Your tender hands. Give me the grace, not to forget, but to move forward in my life. Increase in me the virtues I miss so much in the one who has gone home to You."

For Personal Reflection or Group Sharing
- Write a letter to each person who died who was close to you, expressing your sadness at any faults of yours in the relationship, gratitude for the good, and hope for that person's future and yours.
- Make a general confession of any sins of yours that hurt the deceased ones.
- "You will only feel better when you know he is in a better place." Picture to yourself or make a drawing showing what this better place might be like.

- Picture to yourself Jesus seated in a beautiful place you are familiar with. Let yourself imagine that you are sitting on one side of him. Then see the person who died walking toward you. Jesus wants you to tell each other everything you didn't have time for before the death. Then say goodbye. Watch your loved one leaving, but you remain close to Jesus.

Scripture and Tradition

"Christ Jesus lay in death's strong bands
For our offenses given:
But now at God's right hand he stands
And brings us life from heaven;
Therefore let us joyful be,
And praise the Father thankfully
With songs of Alleluia.
Alleluia. How long and bitter was the strife
When life and death contended,
The victory remained with life,
The reign of death was ended:
Stripped of power, no more it reigns,
And empty form alone remains.
Death's string is lost forever. Alleluia.
So let us keep this festival
To which Our Lord invites us,
The Savior who is joy of all,
The Sun that warms and lights us:
By his grace he shall impart

Eternal sunshine to the heart;

The night of sin has ended.

Alleluia.

> (*Liturgy of the Hours*, "Hymn for Evening Prayer," p. 352)

Many grievers agree with me that after the death of a beloved person the words of Scripture come alive in a new way. As you read the famous passages I have assembled here you might try inserting your own name in each and, where appropriate the name of the one who has left this world, as in the first: "the Lord's kindness has not forsaken the living (you, Ronda) or the dead (Charlie and Martin)." Or "Even though, I, (Ronda) walk through the valley of the shadow of death...."

"(The Lord's) kindness has not forsaken the living or the dead!" (Ruth 2:20)

"Would I had died instead of you. O Absalom, my son, my son!" (2 Samuel 18:33)

"Even though I walk through the valley of the shadow of death, I fear no evil, for thou art with me." (Ps. 23:4)

"Turn thou to me and be gracious to me; for I am lonely and afflicted." (Psalm 25:16)

"The Lord gave, the Lord has taken away; blessed be the name of the Lord." (Job 1:21)

"I know that my Redeemer lives and...after my skin has been thus destroyed, then (from) my flesh I shall see God." (Job 19:25-26)

"He will swallow up death for ever, and the Lord God will wipe away tears from all faces." (Isaiah 25:8)

"For behold, I create new heavens and a new earth, and the former things shall not be remembered or come into mind." (Isaiah 65:17)

"After two days he will revive us; on the third day he will raise us up, that we may live for him." (Hosea 6:2)

"Blessed be the pure of heart, for they shall see God." (Mt. 5:8)

"Blessed are those who mourn, for they shall be comforted." (Mt. 5:5)

"Fear not, therefore, you are of more value than many sparrows." (Mt. 10:31)

"And when I go and prepare a place for you, I will come again and will take you to myself, that where I am you may be also." (John 14:3)

(To the good thief) "Today you shall be with me in paradise" (John 23: 43)

"But Mary (Magdalene) stood weeping outside the tomb…" (John 20:11)

"No one has ascended up to heaven but he who descended from heaven, the Son of man. who is in heaven…that whoever believes in him may have eternal life." (John. 3:13, 15)

"My sheep hear my voice. I know them, and they follow me. I give them eternal life, and they shall never perish. No one shall snatch them out of my hand." (John. 10:27-28)

"In my Father's house there are many rooms…I go to prepare a place for you….I will come again and will take you to myself…" (John. 14:2-3)

"…that your joy may be full." (John. 16:24)

"We know that the whole creation has been groaning in travail together until now, and not only the creation, but we ourselves, who have the first fruits of the Spirit, groan inwardly as we wait for adoption as sons, the redemption of our bodies. For in this hope we were saved. …if we hope for what we do not see, we wait for it with patience."

(Rm. 8:22-25)

"What no eye has seen, nor ear heard, nor the heart of man conceived, what God has prepared for those who love him…" (1 Corinthians 2:9)

"For we now see in a mirror dimly, but then face to face." (1 Corinthians 13:12)

"But if there is no resurrection of the dead, then Christ has not been raised; if Christ has not been raised, then our preaching is in vain…we are of all men most to be pitied." (1 Cor. 15:13-19)

"But some one will ask, 'How are the dead raised? With what kind of body do they come?' You foolish man! What you sow does not come to life unless it dies. And what you sow is not the body which is to be, but a bare kernel, perhaps of wheat or of some other grain. But God gives it a body as he has chosen, and to each kind of seed its own body….So it is with the resurrection of the dead. What is sown is perishable, what is raised is imperishable. It is sown in dishonor, it is raised in glory. It is sown in weakness, it is raised in power. It is sown a physical body, it is raised a spiritual body….Just as we have borne the image of the man of dust, we shall also bear the image of the man of heaven….we shall all be changed, in a moment, in the twinkling of an eye, at the last trumpet. For the trumpet will sound, and the dead will be raised imperishable, and we shall be changed. For his perishable nature must put on the imperishable, and this mortal nature must put on immortality…. 'Death is swallowed up in victory."

(1 Corinthians 15: 35-54)

"So we do not lose heart…this…momentary affliction is preparing for us an eternal weight of glory beyond all comparison, because we look not to the things that are seen but to the things that are unseen; for the things that are seen are transient, but the things that are unseen are eternal. For we know that if the earthly tent we live in is destroyed, we have a building from God, a house not made with hands, eternal in the heavens. Here indeed we groan, and long to put on our heavenly dwelling…He who has prepared us for this very thing is God, who has given us the Spirit as a guarantee...we walk by faith, not by sight."

(2 Corinthians 4: 16-18, 5: 1-7)

"For our commonwealth is in heaven, and from it we await a Savior, the Lord Jesus Christ, who will change our lowly body to be like his glorious body, by the power which enables him even to subject all things to himself." (Philippians 3:20-21)

"Perfect love casts out fear." (1 Jn. 4:18)

"...and God will wipe away every tear from their eyes." (Revelation 7:17)

"And I heard a voice from heaven saying.... 'Blessed are the dead who die in the Lord...that they may rest from their labors, for their deeds follow them!'" (Revelation 14:13)

"And night shall be no more; they need no light of lamp or sun, for the Lord God will be their light, and they shall reign for ever and ever." (Revelation 22:5)

The Catholic faith is based on Scripture and tradition. Under the headings of eternal life, hell, purgatory, heaven, and the resurrected body, you will be provided here with the basic teachings you need for guidance on your journey from grief to hope.

ETERNAL LIFE

When I became a Catholic at age 21 I thought I was pretty well-versed in the fundamentals of the faith. Wrong! Even though every Sunday I recited the words in the Creed, "I believe in the resurrection of the body," somehow I thought that it was the soul that survives death and the body is dead forever.

Over and over again I hear or read words to this effect: "I really can't look forward much to heaven because it is hard to imagine myself liking a place of no movement, no nature, just maybe hymns of angels." Such Christians seem never to have read the prophesy, "Then I saw a new heaven and a new earth." (Revelations 21:01) A good way to picture heaven, I believe, is to think of whatever you have experienced that gave you joy, and then multiply it by a million. And I would certainly include in those times of joy not only love of family and friends but also of the ocean, trees, and flowers.

Even if you truly understand the faith perfectly you will probably still find that in a state of grieving, reading about the promises we believe in about eternal life will bring comfort and added hope.

Before studying our doctrines about specific destinations, let us look at some general truths about eternal life from tradition.

Does the Christian teaching build on what the Jews believed in the Old Testament? You may recall that in the time of Jesus there was controversy with those Sadducees who denied life after death and the Pharisees strongly convinced of it. (see Mark 12:24-26 and Acts 23:6) This is explained partly by the fact that the fullness of eternal life could be opened to the Jews only after the Messiah came. He it was who would reveal the nature of our final destiny.

Many centuries later, after Christ came, among those Jews who did not believe He was the Messiah, there was still uncertainty. But the most respected medieval Jewish philosopher and theologian, Moses Maimonides, in his Thirteen Principles of Faith, wrote that the resurrection of the dead is a basic principle of the Torah of Moses. (See *A Maimonides Reader*, edited by Isidore Twersky. New York: Behrman House, 1972, pp. 401-23.) Maimonides proclaimed that anyone who does not believe in the resurrection of the dead has no connection with the Jewish nation. The resurrection, however, he maintained, is only for the righteous. Maimonides insisted that God's justice entails that with all the sufferings of the just on earth there must be a compensatory world to come. He also wrote about a place of soul cleansing called Gehinnom. After death, those righteous souls know they will be saved, and that they are being prepared for the world to come when they will join the souls that went right after death to the Garden of Eden.

In the *Catechism of the Catholic Church* (#988-1019) we rejoice to see spelled out how the coming of Jesus Christ, the true Messiah, has opened the gates of eternal life, and given us a much clearer sense of what our choices on earth should be to avoid hell and to receive the graces of purgatory and heaven.

I certainly draw hope from these passages from the section of the catechism in explication of the words of the Creed 'I believe in the resurrection...' You might want to read them slowly in a prayerful manner such as adding an Amen after each paragraph or "Thank you, Jesus," or "may it be so for myself and those I love who are now with You."

"We firmly believe, and hence we hope that, just as Christ is truly risen from the dead and lives forever, so after death the righteous will live forever with the risen Christ and he will raise them up on the last day." (#988)

"It is Jesus himself who on the last day will raise up those who have believed in him, who have eaten his body and drunk his blood." (#994)

"...death entered the world on account of man's sin....Death was therefore contrary to the plans of God the Creator and entered the world as a consequence of sin." (#1008)

"Because of Christ, Christian death has a positive meaning: 'For to me to live is Christ, and to die is gain.'" (Philippians 1:21) (#1010)

"In death, God calls man to himself. Therefore the Christian can... transform his own death into an act of obedience and love towards the Father, after the example of Christ." (#1011)

And here are some of my favorite quotations from the saints about eternal life:

"I can never lose one whom I have loved unto the end; one to whom my soul cleaves so firmly that it can never be separated does not go away but only goes before. Be mindful of me when you come to where I shall follow you." (St. Bernard, *Quotable Saints*, p. 47)

71

"Blessed be God for our sister, the death of the body." (St. Francis of Assisi, (*Quotable Saints*, p. 47)

"You, if you are an apostle, will not have to die. You will move to a new house: that is all." (St. Jose Escriva, *Quotable Saints*, p. 51)

Part of the legacy of the Church is the wisdom of holy men and women even if they have not been canonized. I hope you will find these quotations from my dear mentor, Charles Rich, as inspiring as I do:

(After visiting the grave of his dear holy friend Tom Prendergast) "Bernie and I stood on his grave, and we were overcome with a holy kind of envy for his soul, because that soul of his is now completely with Christ, and in that completeness which he always wanted so much."

"God has given us two different modes of communication, one with the living, one with the dead. The dead speak to us and we to them but we do so in the depths of our being which God alone is able to penetrate...there is a certain deep-seated satisfaction whenever we think in a holy way of those who have already left this life."

"We should moderate the sadness we feel when we learn that someone has died by the thought that he has taken a part of ourselves with him...part of us has emigrated to heaven every time someone by means of death goes there ahead of us."

"A saint said that God sometimes gives us our purgatory on this earth, so in losing your son and husband you must have gotten yours. We want to see God immediately on our departure from this life, and so, Ronda dearest, God loves you very much so He will give you the grace to be with and see Him...it is a special sign of God's love to suffer so much."

HELL, PURGATORY AND HEAVEN

In former days the subject of hell was a frequent topic in Christian conversation. Some thought most people went there. Even though the documents of Vatican II and the Catholic Catechism by no means deny hell's reality, there is a tendency among many of us since Vatican II to avoid mention of it in favor of just hoping no one goes there, especially not those we love.

However, in *A Grief Observed*, C.S. Lewis points out that it is not Christian to think that all the dead are at peace. (pp. 24-25) Somewhat wryly, he suggests that since God's love is compatible with Him hurting us on earth why not after death.

"I never believed before – I thought it immensely improbable – that the faithfulest soul could leap straight into perfection and peace the moment death has rattled in the throat. H. was a splendid thing; a soul straight, bright, and tempered like a sword. But not a perfected saint. A sinful woman married to a sinful man; two of God's patients, not yet cured. I know there are not only tears to be dried but stains to be scoured. The sword will be made even brighter." (p. 35)

In *Jaws of Death, Gate of Heaven*, Von Hildebrand wrote that even though we should long to meet Christ in eternity, death is still a fearful reality. Heaven is not automatic for ourselves or those we care about.

"We should be afraid of death because we will be subject to judgment and our illusions will be torn away. Yet we should also have hope that we will one day meet God and in the face of Christ and Mary and the saints and our beloved death, the darkness of death, which is real, can be pierced by the light of faith." (p. ix)

"In death we, and everyone else, have to face judgment, but also will meet Jesus face to face, so we have fear and hope, both so impressive in the liturgies for the dead." (p. 69)

Lest fear for ourselves and those who have gone before overwhelm us, Von Hildebrand includes in his treatise the challenging thought that if we love Jesus we must long to have the bridegroom come even more than we fear judgment. (see p. 80)

Let us go to Scripture and the Catechism for more truth about hell.

In the *Concordance to the Bible*, I found that Jesus warns of hell many times, especially for those who have indifference toward the needy. (See Matthew 25:31-46). Ridicule with its note of sarcastic scorn is also somewhat surprisingly singled out as endangering a person's soul. (Matthew 5:22)

And, the ever popular lust, as well. (Matthew 5:30)

> "The teaching of the Church affirms the existence of hell and its eternity. Immediately after death the souls of those who die in a state of mortal sin descend into hell, where they suffer the punishment of hell...The chief punishment of hell is eternal separation from God, in whom alone man can possess the life and happiness for which he was created and for which he longs."
>
> (*Catechism of the Catholic Church*, #1035)

Does that mean that we should live in dread that any one who died who had not made a last sacramental confession of serious sins is doomed? Certainly, as we shall see in the section of this chapter on purgatory, such a fear is an important reason to frequently and ardently intercede in prayer for the soul of anyone who lived in disobedience to God's law. But we need to also take heed of this teaching:

> "God predestines no one to go to hell; for this, a willful turning away from God (a mortal sin) is necessary, and persistence in it until the end. In the Eucharistic liturgy and in the daily prayers of her faithful, the Church implores the mercy of God, who does not want 'any to perish, but all to come to repentance.'" (#1037)

It is not our job to judge each other concerning final damnation. Many a public sinner still loves God in spite of his or her weaknesses. It used to be pointed out especially at parish missions as an incentive to approaching the sacrament of reconciliation that, besides the Virgin Mary, there is only one person we are told about in Scripture who we know went straight to heaven: a thief and a murderer: the man who prayed to Jesus from his adjacent crucifix.

We must always hope that even if no outward sign was given of repentance before death, a hardened sinner may yet have inwardly turned to God at the last moment. A woman whose husband had lived a sinful life was thrown into despair when this man ended his own life jumping off a bridge into a deep river. St. John Vianney saw in a mystical vision that "between the bridge and the river, he repented and was forgiven." How comforting to his devout widow.

We also need not think that everyone who died outside the Church went to hell. We need to pray for them, but also to bear in mind this teaching: "They could not be saved who, knowing that the Catholic Church was founded as necessary by God through Christ, would refuse either to enter it or to remain in it." (#846) quoting Vatican II, Constitution on the Church, 14.)

Now many people never enter the Church because they are ignorant of our teachings, either never hearing them, or being blocked in understanding by long traditions of anti-Catholicism. Without a special grace it is easier for many to focus, to our shame, on sins of Catholics, past and present, rather than the beauty of the faith itself and its holy sacraments.

God can find ways we do not know of to reach out to his beloved children of other religions or even no religion. (See *Catechism of the Catholic Church*, #847) Having been brought up by atheists, some of whom found the Catholic faith and others did not, I find a contemporary popular theological speculation consoling: at death everyone gets to see the light of Christ. Those who love goodness will move toward him. Those who hate goodness will sink away into the hell they have chosen for themselves. I do not take such a speculation to substitute for The Final Judgement of the Lord.

These questions preoccupied me primarily as my father approached his death. He had been baptized in a Presbyterian Church by his devout mother, but was more influenced by his father – an atheistic Jewish Mason. In his teens he expressed his doubt of God's existence by publically announcing his disbelief as he walked out of the Church forever. During a long life he strove to do good, in sometimes heroic ways, but also flaunted a morality contrary to Christian teaching in other decisions. He was horrified, but also puzzled, when his ex-wife, my mother, and two of his daughters, became Catholics. It was his conviction that all intelligent good people were atheists, like himself.

Because many of the Presidents of the United States had not been Church-goers, he assumed they were also atheists and wrote tracts quoting such passages.

Of course I prayed for him every day and tried to reach him with philosophical arguments for God's existence. Just before he died I happened to be reading a long biography of Abraham Lincoln. I was impressed by how often Lincoln prayed to God even though he didn't attend Church. I put little post-its on each page where Lincoln mentioned God and handed it to my father, then in his eighties. He seemed shook up. On my last visit he shared with tears in his eyes that he was sorry for different people he had hurt during his life. I left a note on his typewriter before I left suggesting he might pray this way: "God, if there is a God, I am grateful to have been given life, and for all the things I enjoyed during my life. I am sorry that I hurt others. If I have a soul, please save me."

When we were sorting out his belongings after his death of cardiac arrest, the note was gone. So, I think he read it, and hope he prayed it.

PURGATORY

When I was a new Catholic on my way from the subway to the office I was working at in New York City, I passed each day a sizable building with a plaque next to the door. On it were the strange words "Helpers of the Poor Souls." Inside was a convent full of contemplative sisters devoted to praying for the souls in purgatory. "Golly, gee," I thought, "those souls must be suffering terribly if they need whole orders of living Catholics to pray for them night and day!"

In the pre-Vatican II Church it was taken for granted that few Christians went right to heaven, and many souls certainly needed our prayers in their journey through purgatory. Even though on All Soul's Day there are still prayers for the souls in purgatory and special graces for those who visit their graves, throughout the year there is much less emphasis on this ministry of hope and love. Possibly also, outspoken rejection of the doctrine by some Protestant Christian groups has left Catholics uncertain.

I have found praying for the souls of my beloved dead is one of the best things I can do. It gives me a positive way to do something with my grief and also a way to do penance for my sins against them. So, in case you are not already praying for your dead often, I am including here Scripture and tradition about purgatory. At the end of this book there will be a small chapter devoted to different prayers, traditional and contemporary, we can say for our dead.

Here are key passages from the *Catechism of the Catholic Church* about purgatory with the Scriptures related to each teaching:

"All who die in God's grace and friendship, but still imperfectly purified, are indeed assured of their eternal salvation; but after death they undergo purification, so as to achieve the holiness necessary to enter the joy of heaven." (*CCC*, #1030)

The Church gives the name Purgatory to this final purification of the elect, which is entirely different from the punishment of the damned.

The Church formulated her doctrine of faith on Purgatory especially at the Councils of Florence and Trent. The tradition of the Church, by reference to certain texts of Scripture, speaks of a cleansing fire.

"If any man's work is burned up, he will suffer loss, though he himself will be saved, but only as through fire." (1 Corinthians 3:15) "...so that the genuineness of your faith, more precious than gold which though perishable is tested by fire, may redound to praise and glory and honor at the revelation of Jesus Christ." (1 Peter 7)

Here is the text quoted in the Catechism from the *Dialogues of St. Gregory the Great*:

"As for certain lesser faults, we must believe that, before the Final Judgment, there is a purifying fire. He who is truth says that whoever utters blasphemy against the Holy Spirit will be pardoned neither in this age nor in the age to come. From this sentence we understand that certain offenses can be forgiven in this age, but certain others in the age to come." (*CCC*, #1031)

"This teaching is also based on the practice of prayer for the dead...(in the Old Testament) 'Therefore (Judas Maccabeus) made atonement for the dead, that they might be delivered from their sin.' (2 Maccabees 12:46) From the beginning the Church has honored the memory of the dead and offered prayers...for them, above all the Eucharistic sacrifice, so that, thus purified, they may attain the beatific vision of God. The Church also commends almsgiving, indulgences, and works of penance undertaken on behalf of the dead." (*CCC*, #1032)

In Martin Barrack's book *Eternal Israel* (unpublished manuscript - footnotes 202-212) there are these references to purgatory cited from the early Church: It is believed that prayers for the souls of those who had gone before were found in the catacombs and also in the Acts of Paul and

Thecla, 160 AD.

Tertullian (155-250 AD) thought that Hades is a place where those with light offenses expiate their sins. He refers to Mt. 5:25 about the judge and the last penny to be paid as related to expiation in purgatory.

St. Cyprian of Carthage (200-258 AD) wrote,

"It is one thing to stand for pardon, another thing to attain to glory; it is one thing, when cast into prison, not to go out thence until one has paid the uttermost farthing; another thing at once to receive the wages of faith and courage. It is one thing, tortured by long suffering for sins, to be cleansed and long purged by fire; another to have purged all sins by suffering. It is one thing, in fine, to be in suspense till the sentence of God at the day of judgment; another to be at once crowned by the Lord."

This purging is also mentioned by St. John Chyrsostom, 344-407 AD: "Let us not hesitate to help those who have died and offer our prayers for them."

Augustine says that the fire of purgatory is more severe than any suffering in this life and that the practice of praying for the dead handed down by the Fathers – they are always mentioned in the Mass.

I especially like this quotation from the writings on purgatory of St. Catherine of Genoa:

"I do not believe it would be possible to find any joy comparable to that of a soul in purgatory, except the joy of the blessed in paradise – a joy which goes on increasing day by day as God more and more flows in upon the soul, which he does abundantly in proportion as every hindrance to his entrance is consumed away."

(Quotable Saints, p. 48)

On a website of Maria Compton-Hernandez of The Catholic Mother's Internet Connection I found these helpful ways of forming a general understanding what purgatory means for our beloved dead.

"The Church consists of three parts working together: The Church Militant (we, those who fight daily for our salvation on earth), the Church Suffering (the Poor Souls in Purgatory), and the Church Triumphant (the Angels and Saints in Heaven). All three branches of the Church make up the Mystical Body of Christ and work together to maintain its foundation. When we, the Church Militant, forget to pray for our suffering brothers and sisters in Purgatory (the Church Suffering), we weaken the foundation of the Church.

"Our Protestant brothers and sisters in Christ insist that there are only two options after death, Heaven and Hell. I am thankful to be Catholic because it gives me the very reassuring knowledge that there is another option after death, one for which most of us should be most grateful: Purgatory. I would be quite afraid to ever assume that I am pure enough to go straight to Heaven after death. It is the Mercy of God which gives humanity a place of purification prior to Heaven: Purgatory. The need for Purgatory can be explained quite easily by using an analogy that I've used to explain this doctrine to my young children. It is a suitable analogy for explaining Purgatory to adults, too.

"Imagine this: you were invited to attend a grand ball, a wonderful party, and everyone there was wearing their finest clothes, had their hair done up beautifully, had been bathed and were clean and sweet-smelling. The host of the party answers the door and you are invited to enter. But you are standing there in horrible rags. Your hair is tangled and smelly, and you are un-clean and need a bath. Would you want to enter into that party?

"For those who continue to insist that there is no Purgatory, I ask: What makes you so sure that you will arrive totally pure, in a sinless state, at the moment of death and judgment? Aren't all of us sinners, daily performing countless small sins which only the eyes of God can see? Be joyful, then, for a place or purgation where we can cleanse ourselves of sin prior to entering into the perfect beauty of Heaven!"

Maria Compton-Hernandez goes on to remind us that, "Through the centuries, Our Lord has granted to many saints and holy chosen individuals the gift of a charism which allows one to be visited by the Souls in Purgatory. Among them are St. Gertrude, St. Catherine of Genoa,… St. Margaret Mary of Paray-le-Monial, the Cure of Ars, St. John Bosco and Blessed Faustina."

Most amazing to me of the accounts of 20th century mystics is that described in the popular book *Get Us Out of Here!* Maria Simmas speaks with Nicky Eltz (The Medjugorje BiH, 2002). From youth Maria Simmas received visions and locutions from the souls in purgatory asking for prayers. There is documentation of many relatives living on earth asking Maria to pray for the souls of their family and friends with signs they could understand as coming directly from the one on the purgatorial journey.

You may think, well God knows the needs of the souls in purgatory; why does He need our prayers? I think of our prayers in analogy to a mother who invites a small child to help her make a cake. She doesn't need the assistance of the child, but she wants to increase its value by having it be a communal project. This builds love in the family. Since heaven will not be each of us alone with God but the joyful reunion of all those who chose the kingdom, through our prayers He allows us to have a part in the grateful happiness of His other children.

To continue with the web-site summary of our teaching on purgatory by Maria Compton Hernandez,

"The most efficacious practice we can do is to have Masses celebrated for the Holy Souls, or for a particular soul who has died. Of course, one should be present at these Masses. Other pious practices which are beneficial to the Holy Souls are saying the Rosary and making the Stations of the Cross on behalf of the Poor Souls. We should never underestimate the value of personal suffering, whether it be physical, spiritual or temporal. Uniting even the tiniest suffering, inconvenience or act of mortification with the sufferings of Jesus and placing them into the hands of the Blessed Mother on behalf of the Poor Souls is another very vital way to assist them.

"This practice used to be called "offering things up" and I have found it a wonderful way to cope with the inevitable frustrations and sufferings of each day. Here are other practices which can assist in aiding the Poor Souls on their journey to Heaven:

- Adoration of the Blessed Sacrament for at least 1/2 hour
- Reading Holy Scripture for at least 1/2 hour
- A church visit between noon of Nov. 1 and midnight of Nov. 2 (Feast of All Souls) for the intentions of the deceased
- Visiting a cemetery for the intentions of the deceased"

"When they are finally released from their pains and enjoy the beatitude of Heaven, far from forgetting their friends on earth, their gratitude knows no bounds. Prostrate before the Throne of God they never cease to pray for those who have helped them. By their prayers they shield their friends from the dangers and protect them from the evils that threaten them.

They will never cease these prayers until they see their bene-factors safely in Heaven. If Catholics only knew what powerful protectors they secure by helping the Holy Souls they would not be so remiss in praying for them."

Compton-Hernandez adds these spiritual teachings:

"Our Lady visits the Souls in Purgatory often to console them and give them encouragement. The Souls refer to her as Mother of Mercy. A single act of charity done in pure love can cover a multitude of sins and decrease significantly our stay in Purga-tory! For as long as we are living on earth we can repair for the evil we have done. We can no longer gain such merits in Purga-tory. Only when we achieve Heaven will we see the number of souls that were saved by accepting our sufferings on earth with patience and uniting them for the Poor Souls with the sufferings of Christ."

A priest once taught me to pray to the angels for the souls of mem-bers of my family. He believed that they love to guide the holy souls from purgatory into heaven. I tried praying in this way for a month. Afterwards I had a sense of peace about the soul of my son.

HEAVEN

The dearest dream of all of us for ourselves and everyone we love is to finally reach heaven, also called paradise. In our times, the concept of heaven, paradise, and, sometimes Eden, are often applied to much lesser realities. A most tragic-comical use I came upon was this one. A friend was taken speedily to a convalescent home after surgery. Given an address in a neighboring town, I expected to see the usual several story outwardly pleasant buildings where the recovering are tended. Arriving I found a scrubby piece of land ungraced by trees, plants, or flowers, but instead with a huge metal garbage dump. On it stood a large white stucco house with pieces of broken plaster around the entrance and a big sign: LITTLE EDEN.

We are accustomed to think blithely of a heavenly ice cream flavor, paradise as a swim in a backyard pool, etc. etc. etc. One of my students announced that he would not want to go to any heaven where his pet dog was not there, as well.

With this in mind, I was pleased to read in C.S. Lewis that the Scriptural view of heaven is not some cozy family reunion that is just like one on earth. We must want God as the end of all our desires, not just think of Him as a means for meeting the beloved dead. (*A Grief Observed*, p. 54)

Actually, I have found a large spectrum of views about what heaven will be like. Some believe we will be caught up in a trance-like state of the vision of God such that we will experience nothing but His absolute, unchanging, immaterial being. And all the way on the other end there are those who want to have everything they enjoyed on earth, even plenty of work to do.

Needless to say, our sense of what we hope for our beloved ones in eternity will be much influenced by such theories, so it is important to see what the Church teaches, based on Scripture and tradition.

"Those who die in God's grace and friendship and are perfectly purified live forever with Christ...(they see him) face to face." (*CCC*, #1023)

> "This perfect life with the Most Holy Trinity – this communion of life and love with the Trinity, with the Virgin Mary, and angels and all the blessed – is called 'heaven.' Heaven is the ultimate end and fulfillment of the deepest human longings, the state of supreme, definite happiness." (*CCC*, #1024)

"The elect live 'in Christ,' but they retain, or rather find, their true identity, their own name." (Revelation 2:17) (*CCC*, #1025)

"The life of the blessed consists in the full and perfect possession of the fruits of the redemption accomplished by Christ. He makes partners in his heavenly glorification those who have believed in him and remained faithful to his will. Heaven is the blessed community of all who are perfectly incorporated into Christ." (*CCC*, #1026)

Note that in these paragraphs we find both the concept of the beatific vision of the Godhead and also a communion with other blessed ones.

And in the final passage in this part of the Catechism you may even find room for your favorite pets: "In the glory of heaven the blessed continue joyfully to fulfill God's will in relation to other men and to all creation." (*CCC*, #1029)

Here are some quotations reflecting the joys to be expected in heaven: (written by St. Stephen in 1109 about the death of a monk friend)

"Alberic is dead to our eyes, but not to the eyes of God. Dead as he seems to us, he lives for us before the Lord. For this is the way of the saints, that when they go to God by death…they carry their friends with them in their heart, there to preserve them forever; so that we may say that, death having united him to God, by an eternal and unchangeable love, he has taken us with him to God." (*Ratisbonne,* St. Bernard, p. 41)

St. Augustine, City of God: 22:30 Vol. 18 Great Books of the Western World (Chicago: *Encyclopedia Brittanica,* 1952) "There we shall rest and see, see and love, love and praise. This is what shall be in the end without end."

St. Gregory the Great wrote:

"So our Lord's sheep will finally reach their grazing ground where all who follow him in simplicity of heart will feed on the green pastures of eternity. These pastures are the spiritual joys of heaven. There the elect look upon the face of God with unclouded vision and feast at the banquet of life for ever more...let us set out for these pastures where we shall keep joyful festival with so many of our fellow citizens. May the thought of their happiness urge us on! Let us stir up our hearts, rekindle our faith, and long eagerly for what heaven has in store for us. To love thus is to be already on our way. No matter what obstacles we encounter, we must not allow them to turn us aside from the joy of that heavenly feast. Anyone who is determined to reach this destination is not deterred by the roughness of the road that leads to it."

(*Office of Readings*, pp. 560-561)

Jesus is said to have told St. Gertrude the Great "my heaven would not be complete without you." (*Quotable Saints*, p. 47)

"My understanding was lifted up into heaven, where I saw our Lord like a lord in his own house who has called all his valued servants and friends to a solemn feast...and (Christ) filled (the house) with joy and mirth. He himself endlessly gladdened and solaced his valued friends...with the marvelous melody of endless love in his own fair, blessed face. This glorious countenance of the godhead completely fills all heaven with joy and bliss...God showed three degrees of bliss that every soul that has willingly served God...shall have in heaven. The first is the gratitude...he shall receive from our Lord god...the second is that all the blessed creatures who are in heaven shall see the glorious thanking...the third...is that is shall last forever."

(Blessed Julian of Norwich *Quotable Saints* p. 48)

"I saw myself dying with a desire to see God, and I knew not how to seek that life other than by dying. Over my spirit flash and float in divine radiancy the bright and glorious visions of the world to which I go."

(St. Teresa of Avila, *Quotable Saints,* p. 49)

The Resurrection of the Body Transfiguration

Old match
in your dusty box who would guess
that struck by human hand you could yet burst into flame?
Old body
in your fatigues who would guess
that in the monstrance of God's love
you could shine with glory?

I wrote this little poem once while meditating on the resurrection of the body. I still like it.

At the start of this chapter I mentioned that some Christians scarcely think about the resurrection of the body, imagining instead a disembodied soul alone even after the Last Judgment. Some of the confusion comes naturally. Since our human minds are such that we can only imagine things that have length and width, depth, and shape, we tend to add these elements even to beings we know to be non-physical. The soul used to be depicted in art as a tiny little human body. When we think of the souls in purgatory it is hard not to have an image of them in the bodies they had on earth. Michelangelo's Creation shows God, who is really pure Spirit, as a majestic figure with a body. Angels, also pure spirits, manifest themselves to humans in visitations in physical form.

Knowing that such pictures are false, we may think that the idea of a resurrected bodies in heaven is also false, forgetting that it is a doctrine of the faith proclaimed every Sunday in the Creed!

"In death, the separation of the soul from the body, the human body decays and the soul goes to meet God, while awaiting its reunion with its glorified body…through the power of Jesus' Resurrection." (*CCC*, #997)

An idea of this glorified body is given us by the accounts of Jesus in his appearances after He rose from the dead. His resurrected body could go through locked doors and also be penetrated by the fingers of doubting Thomas; he could eat, and also be visibly lifted into heaven at the Ascension.

Some quotations from the Fathers of the Church may help you delve into this great mystery:

"Indeed, God calls even the body to resurrection, and promises it everlasting life. When He promises to save the man, He thereby makes His promise to the flesh: for what is man but a rational living being composed of soul and body? Is the soul by itself a man? No, it is but the soul of a man. Can the body be called a man? No, it can but be called the body of a man. If then, neither of these is by itself a man, but that which is composed of the two together is called a man, and God has called man to life and resurrection, He has called not a part, but the whole, which is the soul and the body."

(St. Justin the Martyr from *The Faith of the Early Fathers*,

Volume 1, p. 63)

"It is more difficult to initiate that which is not, than to repeat that which has been. Do you think that if something be withdrawn from our feeble eyes, it perishes to God? Everybody, whether it withers into dust or is dissolved into moisture or is crumbled into ashes or passes off as a vapor, is removed from our eyes; but a guard is kept over its elements by God….See, too, how for our consolation all nature suggests the future resurrection. The sun sinks down, but is reborn. The stars go out, but return again. Flowers die, but come to life again. After their decay shrubs put forth leaves again...A body in the grave is like the trees in winter: they hide their sap under a deceptive dryness. Why are you in haste for it to revive and return, while yet the winter is raw? We must await even the spring of the body..."

(Minucius Felix, from *The Faith of the Early Fathers*, Volume 1, p. 110)

"To the good man to die is gain. The foolish, fear death as the greatest of evils, the wise desire it as a rest after labors and the end of life." (St. Ambrose, *Quotable Saints*, p. 46)

"The bodies of the saints will rise again free from every defect, from every deformity, as well as from every corruption, encumbrance, or hindrance. In this respect their freedom of action will be as complete as their happiness." (St. Augustine, *Quotable Saints*, p. 46)

And here is a heartening passage from the last sermon of a martyr, St. Fidelis, a 16th century priest of Switzerland: "What made the holy apostles and martyrs endure fierce agony and bitter torments, except faith, and especially faith in the resurrection? Most of us will not by martyrs, but we have agony and torment in our grief and shall we not also have hope?" (*Office of Readings*, p. 1391)

For personal reflection or group sharing:
- Have your concepts of eternal life, hell, purgatory, heaven and the resurrected body changed over time? How?
- Have the ideas in this chapter been new to you?
- You might want to draw a picture of each of your beloved dead situating them in eternity or write a personal prayer for those ones journeying the beyond.

Living in the Lord
"until we meet again."

"Thou who hast made me see many sore troubles, Wilt revive me again; from the depths of the earth thou wilt bring me up again. Thou wilt increase my honor, and comfort me again."

(Psalm 71: 20-21)

"We know that in everything God works for good with those who love him, who are called according to his purpose."

(Romans 8:28)

"In some marvelous and ineffable way we are now already the way we will be in heaven, loving that in each other which we will take with us when we leave this world, our deep inner being. And, loving that in each other, we can also have each other, though we are separated from each other physically."

(Charles Rich – "Give me your Heart" –
Preparing for Eternal Life)

At the time of the death of a loved one it is usually almost impossible to believe that anything good in our lives can balance the sorrow. Yet, this image from our widow, Sue Norris, reflects how in spite of feeling broken to bits, God does plan to bring good out of tragedy: "As I looked at my life, all it seemed to consist of was a collection of fragments, not a coherent whole. The pieces of myself that are left over have to be reworked…the potter and the clay of Jeremiah 18:4? He is forming us into new persons… is it not resurrection to receive at his hands a new life?" (*Holding Hands with God*, pp. 55-57)

I met Sue Norris at the Franciscan University of Steubenville when I was a new widow, and it soothed me to think that I was clay being re-formed by the hands of my Jesus. The new life is in continuity with the person we were before the death. We read about St. Clotilda and we see that she is still all-mother after her child left the world:

"I give thanks to Almighty God that He has not considered me un-worthy to be the mother of a child admitted into the celestial kingdom. Having quitted the world in the white robe of his innocence, he will rejoice in the presence of God through all eternity." (*Quotable Saints*, p. 47)

This poem, written by my mother in her old age, illustrates the way many of us feel, bereft after a death, yet still able to respond to new calls:

Old and Alone
"Without love
She said
The flesh shrivels
The mind dulls
The heart dies
But, my dear,
This is the human condition
At your time of life
You know that.
You must turn to God.
He alone is always there

And loves you.

Yes –ah, yes – God

But God has no arms to put around me

No hands to clasp in mine or stroke my hair

No chest on which to rest my head

No wit to set my mind to dancing

No sudden smile to pierce my heart with love

No lips to kiss

No body to join with mine in union…

Don't you see?

Don't you understand?

I am drowning in a sea of loneliness

I need a living, breathing human being

To love and call my own.

You long for what you can no longer have

Take pleasure in what you still have left…

Eyes to see the lovely light of sun on grass

Ears to hear the music of a child's laugh

Pass along a word of wisdom to one who needs it

Hold a sobbing child to your breast…

You supply to someone else the very things you miss.

Give your arms, your hands, your wit, your smile.

A close embrace to warm another's frozen soul.

Revive another's dying heart.

It is the lonely who must help the lonely."

Helen Winner (*Seeking Christ in the Crosses and Joys of Aging* by Ronda Chervin, (Oak Lawn, Illinois: CMJ Marian Publishers, 2000) pp. 31-32.

Here is a stunning example by Hillel Fendel of a Jewish man bereft of his son spending his time "until we meet again," in an extraordinary ministry of helping others (from a Website Designed for "Bringing out the Good" May 9, 2006)

"Rafi Sofer, 75, of Oranit (near Petach Tikvah), experienced the tragedy of his son's suicide - and decided to use it to spread happiness and joy to others.

"After undergoing months of total despair and sorrow, Rafi's son appeared to him in a dream - and he then resolved to open a website featuring happy and positive stories....

"Until you experience something like your son dying, you cannot understand to what depths you can fall," Rafi said. "My son's death totally shattered me. I had nightmares every night." But one night, several months ago, everything changed.

"My son Guy appeared to me in a dream," Rafi told HaTzofeh's Yaffa Goldstein. "He was calm and serene like he never was in his lifetime. He hugged me and showed me a heart, on one side of which was written rak [only], and on the other was written tov [good]. I understood that he was giving me a message and that I had to act accordingly. The next morning I started the website."

"The site is as its name implies - only good stories, "an answer to the violence, treachery, and corruption we always read about. It's no wonder that the youth, exposed to such terrible things, like to close themselves up, and that sometimes those of them who are more sensitive and deep are willing to give up everything."

"Rafi turned down an offer from Microsoft Israel to partner with the "Good-Only" site, saying, "My purpose is to eternalize my son, and it can't be commercialized or polluted by those types of ads."

"It appears that the one that gives him (Rafi) the most satisfaction is meeting people and bringing out the good in them. He says that the purpose of the site is to "encourage people, especially youth and children, to publicize stories of good deeds."

"One story on the site is of two 60-year-old cousins who happily discovered each other for the first time by virtue of a photograph of their mutual grandmother displayed in a hospital exhibit...

"One 10-year-old boy tells...that he and his brother take turns sleeping at their widowed grandmother's home "so that she won't be alone."

"Rafi Sofer sums up: 'I think that if I sit with the youth, talk to them and give them a tool by which to emphasize the good, this will help them to be less pressured and tense. Maybe I'm naive, but if my talks and efforts to uncover the good prevent just one act of suicide, I will be happy.'"

As in the above story, God can use a death as a kind of wake-up call. Before my son committed suicide, my husband, Martin, had the family and a few close friends, but was otherwise rather isolated – devoting himself in the later years of his life to writing (see Bibliography for some of his wonderful works). He became a Catholic when he was 60 years old, but insisted he didn't want to be a daily-Mass Catholic like me. His spirituality was what is sometimes called vertical – related mostly to God, not to love of neighbor and he hated the handshake of peace at Mass as something artificial and distracting.

After Charlie's death, however, he found in his grief that it was only at daily Mass that he could find any hope. The dead don't run away from us, so much as we run toward them – toward eternity. So Martin began to go with me each day to Church, offering his holy communion with these words: "cover the naked soul of my son with Your Body and Blood."

My daughter, Diana, wrote him a poem about his whole life shortly before his own death with these lines at the end:

"A man can see his son's strong light grow dim – a man can give of all he is to save it –
a man can climb in darkness through the narrow paths, screaming within his soul with all his might.
A man can give up sleep for many nights, and face the day resolved to win the fight –
a man can hold his son's small face within both hands, and breathe like the Creator on the clay.
a man can hold his breath and whisper a last prayer, and let go, praying he is doing right....
There is a horror in the letting go,
Insanity lies grimacing around every corner –
And how can you say 'Rest in pace, my only son'
And not remember Isaac, innocent, before the slaughter. There is true misery in going on –
Impossible you say – And yet I do;
Surrounded by my dreams of him, Living for some sign from him, Weeping at night
Counting the days –
Amazed and appalled that so much time is passed –
At last, a show world of nothing held between my hands –
Reaching heavenward with nought but hope,
Begging God
'Please, please, my boy, my life' Groping for patience,
Groping for belief...
An unheard voice whispers with pride 'You are my son!
And you will see great wonders, yet,
Believe it, and hold the hands of both your son and mine...."

Not only did Charlie's death bring my husband closer to Jesus, now his only hope, but also closer even to strangers. There was an elderly brother and sister who sat in front of us each day at Mass. I heard that the woman had Alzheimers. At the time of the greeting of peace, Martin offered only the most perfunctory handshake to them. But, after a year of daily Mass, one day Martin noticed that the sister was not present. After Mass he introduced himself and with real concern asked the brother how his sister was. He also reached out to a couple in the parish who were in marital crisis.

If these anecdotes, rather than advancing toward a definite conclusion, seem kind of circular, there is a reason. Paradoxically, the loss of a loved one can bring us closer to God, but then that closeness helps us love human persons in a deeper more spiritual way.

In *Jaws of Death: Gate of Heaven,* Von Hildebrand explains that "Our ultimate theme as human beings is not union with another person (however strong our love may be), but union with Jesus and, in Him and through Him, union with God the Father." (p. 52)

"True human love is a foretaste of eternity 'the blissful glance of mutual love must be eternal, otherwise it would be nothing." (*Jaws of Death*, p. 97)

After Charlie's death Jesus seemed to tell me that he wanted me to find Charlie only in Him because that would draw me closer to him every day in deep prayer. He wants me to be holy because just as I am longing for Charlie, so He is longing for intimacy with me!

Charles Rich wrote: "As we advance in years, people leave us, and this is a blessing, since we have more time to be with God."

"'His or her soul is Mine not yours,' God says of those He takes by means of a holy and happy death. We should in no way complain in that those we love go back to God from whom they came...we should say with the Psalmist: 'I rejoiced when they said to me: we will go up to the house of the Lord,' meaning by these words that everyone must leave this life."

In this spirit we understand these words of the mother we cited earlier who wrote about her miscarriage:

"I at least knew that my daughter was safe with God, and that nothing in this world could ever hurt her again. We named her Christina Grace. It just didn't feel right not to give her a name, although she would never need it in this world, even for a tombstone. We would never see her, never hold her, never help her to grow in love and holiness, but at least we could give her a name. We had a Mass celebrated in her honor…as a rite of passage…It helped us to accept that our child was in heaven, that our love for her and delight in her existence had been received, and that God, in his infinite mercy and love, had received this precious child of ours in his arms and was now holding her to his bosom…(miscarried babies) are a sort of anchor for the rest of us still on this earth…they are waiting to welcome us home to heaven. Now death brings something concretely joyful with it – the reunion with those little ones."

Katherine O'Brien-Johnston,
(*Holding Hands with God* pp. 75-78)

CHOICES: THE SAINTS LEAD THE WAY

Of course, the death of a loved, even a spouse, does not mean that our own life ends. Grief assumes a place within a life that goes on and what goes on in that life has a lot to do with the bearing of grief. After a death, weeping with Jesus will always be part of our lives, but spending most of our time in brooding is one of the worst way to cope with grief. And this brings up many choices, especially where the death means a change in life-style.

The choices I understand the best are choices widows can make and, of course, these choices are also open to widowers, with the added possibility of a late vocation to the priesthood! But, many a parent grieving over the death of a child, has important choices to make. Should I volunteer to help hospitalized children? Many an elderly person who has lost siblings will want to work afterwards with agencies such as hospice. Those bereaved when they are still relatively young will train for paid work in areas of help.

When I researched the widow saints for my book *A Widow's Walk: Encouragement, Comfort, and Wisdom from the Widow Saints* (Huntington, Indiana, Our Sunday Visitor, 1998), I divided the choices of the widows into these: Remarriage, Helping the Needy, Intercessory Pilgrims, often Penitents, Prophetesses, Contemplatives, sisters and Nuns, and Foundresses. Becoming part of the on-going revival of Consecrated Widowhood is also a possibility. Since this book is now out of print, I will summarize some of the stories of these holy widows. Even if the death you are grieving is not that of your spouse, you may want to read about these brave widows, for their lives are interesting adventures in grace. As you read consider what the Holy Spirit might be telling you.

The possibility of remarriage was considered by some saints, and usually rejected in favor of having Jesus as the Second Bridegroom. However, one of the most famous of all saints remarried after the death of a spouse: St. Thomas More.

In her book *By Grief Refined*, Alice Von Hildebrand, the widow of the famous philosopher Dietrich Von Hildebrand, explains that when a marriage was based on a great love, the idea of remarriage is repugnant. In the case of a less than perfect union of hearts there may be reason to consider marrying again, or because of the needs of the children.

One of the major occupations of the widow saints who had children was what we now call single-parenting. This was sometimes made easier by their extended family life-style, but not always. St. Jane of Chantal, for example, to preserve the inheritance of her children, had to live in the home of her father-in-law, whose household was run by his mistress! Rejection by the family and poorer living conditions was the plight of such saints as Elizabeth Seton and Marguerite d'Youville.

One of the widow saints most often noted for care of the needy was St. Elizabeth of Hungary (1207-1231). After a deeply happy and spiritual marriage, Elizabeth, a princess, was left a widow at a very young age with small children. A Third Order Franciscan, she divested herself as soon as possible of the luxuries she enjoyed as a noble woman and used her last resources to set up a nursing home for the destitute.

A more recent example of a widow who devoted herself to helping the poor was Praxedes Fernandez of Spain (1886-1936) Left a widow with still young children, she had no place to go but her mother's house. A single sister, who disliked having boisterous young boys in the home, tried to keep Praxedes and her children from moving back into the family household. She insisted that if Praxedes returned it would have to be as a servant. With holy sacrificial love, the saint agreed, tending everyone in the family in the role of maid. At the end of her life she became a minister of peace by bringing food to the hungry whether they be Catholics or Communists. A leftist revolutionary claimed that if all Catholics were like Praxedes there would be no communists. (See Martin-Maria Olive, *Praxedes: Wife, Mother, Widow and Lay Dominican.*)

How many widows and widowers are to be found helping in the Vincent de Paul Society, at soup kitchens, hospices, women's shelters, and other places.

The option of becoming an intercessor, penitent, or pilgrim, or all three at the same time has been and is still now more popular than you might imagine. Think of how many older women are to be seen praying the rosary in the parish, volunteering for Eucharistic adoration, or making pilgrimages to national or international shrines or apparition sites.

A spectacular example of such a life-style is Blessed Angela of Foligno (1248-1309). A married woman with children who was also an adulteress, Angela had a stunning conversion experience. After the death of her husband and children to the plague, she moved into a hut with a woman companion and began a life of penance and mystical prayer, broken by occasional pilgrimages to nearby Assisi. A key factor in her painful but often also ecstatic visions was a union with Jesus as her true bridegroom redolent of sentiments transfigured from her earlier passions. Her sayings, taken down by cleric disciples, had a great influence on contemplative prayer throughout the centuries since her death. (See Angela of Foligno: Complete Works)

An intercessor, mystic, and what we would call today a prophetess, was the fourteenth century St. Birgitta of Sweden (see Jorgensen, Saint Bridget of Sweden). She is most well-known today because her visions and meditations on the Passion of Christ played a role in the film of that name produced by Mel Gibson. Happily married to a devout member of the noble classes in Sweden, and mother of many children, after the death of her spouse, she went on a long pilgrimage to Rome where she made her way from church to church in prayer with a following of disciples.

Two of the most significant contemplative saints in the history of the Church were widows. Blessed Marie of the Incarnation was a 17th century contemplative and missionary from France to the natives of Canada. The part that has always amazed me is that her highest visions of the Lord took place while she was watering down the horses after their labor in carting goods from ship to town. This job in her in-laws carting business she was too poor to refuse. (see *Marie of the Incarnation: Selected Writings*)

An extraordinary widow mystic I have already cited in this book is Conchita of Mexico. As a wife and mother of nine, she had plenty of practical things to do during the day. God led Conchita, a 20th century contemplative, to pray during the night, recording what she heard in her heart. The total of her writings before becoming a widow and after come to more than a hundred volumes – these being translated into English one by one in our times. I believe that someday she will be declared a doctor of the Church.

Although Jesus told her to remain in the world she founded an order to cloistered nuns and also helped found the Missionaries of the Holy Spirit and a few other active communities. When I asked a priest follower of hers how her spirituality differed from that of Little Therese of Lisieux, he said that she was more motherly. Many a widow in our times, without becoming part of a contemplative community, enjoy spending many of the hours she previously spent with her husband, in quiet deep prayer, especially adoration of Jesus in the Blessed Sacrament.

Some widows became religious sisters such as St. Rita of Cascia, who lived in Italy from 1381-1457. When her sons died in an epidemic, Rita tried three times to enter a particular monastery. She stripped herself of all her belongings to be ready to enter at a moment's notice. Rita was refused because of her age. Then in a miraculous occurrence, the saint was transported by heavenly saints past the locked gate of the convent into a choir stall. Although many widows would find it difficult to be obedient to sometimes younger administrators in a religious community, some are able to do so. A community that accepts older as well as younger women is the Handmaids of Nazareth.

The same skills needed in running a household can come to the fore in the founding of new religious communities. Among the widow saints who founded new orders the one best known to the English-speaking world is St. Elizabeth Seton (1774-1821), an American saint. She agreed to found the first order for teaching Sisters only when the Bishop allowed her to keep her daughters with her. The sons studied at a boarding school in Maryland, not too far away.

Mary, the Mother of Jesus, is not always thought of as a widow with choices to make. In many ways her life after the death of Joseph spans all the options of the other widow saints, except, of course, penance for personal sin.

Surely the widow Mary extended arms of compassion to the needy, interceded with all her heart for the brothers and sisters in the fledgling

Church and dwelled in contemplative prayer. How many religious orders bear her name!

A litany prayer to Mary, Exalted Widow, can be found in the last chapter of this book: Prayers for the Dead.

For more information on the widow saints, visit www.rondachervin. com for a PDF of my out-of-print book or try to find it at used book web sites. For smaller stories of these saints go to my *Treasury of Women Saints*.

You might want to know about an on-going revival of consecrated widows. In the New Testament we read about different types of widows: gossipy, drunken ones, and others who lived only for Christ and the Church. (See 1 Timothy 5:3-16) The latter formed an order of widows, the first consecrated women in the early Church. Gradually over time such consecrated women were assumed into the religious orders of nuns and sisters.

Since Vatican II there has been a movement to revive consecrated widows. There are presently such consecrated widows in France, Italy, Spain, Poland and Czechoslovakia, but not yet in the United States.

The Vatican is working on a rite for consecrated widows. This would not be a group living together (though consecrated widows could choose to live in a group) but rather individuals who want to live much as did the consecrated widows described in the New Testament, either alone or in their families. In preparation for this possibility, I am living my life as a widow within the home of one of my daughters with this informal rule:

- Private promise not to remarry ever (any priest can receive such a promise)
- Simple life – giving everything away to the poor I don't need as a necessity. (An example of something that is not a luxury for me would be having money around to travel to see my grandchildren.)
- Daily Mass and frequent Confession.
- Daily Rosary.
- Chaplet of Divine Mercy.

- Prayer from the Liturgy of the Hours and Office of Readings and other spiritual readings.
- Silent prayer – adoration or in my little oratory at home.

I devote most of my time to apostolic endeavors such as speaking, writing and teaching. I am not under strict obedience, but I do follow the advice of my priest spiritual director and my pastor. If you are a devout widow you might want to pray about a life-style for yourself that you would want to try with the help of a spiritual director or pastor. (Cardinal Raymond Burke, who oversaw this emerging possibility in the United States, once suggested that widows who feel called to a consecrated life as individuals should write a letter expressing their reasons to the Congregation in Rome working on a possible rite: His Excellency Francis Cardinal Arinze Congregation of Divine Worship and the Discipline of the Sacraments 00120 Vatican City State, Europe.)

THE LONGING OF THE HUMAN HEART FOR GOD

Let me return now to universal themes of those who have lost loved ones, not specifically widows. What more can be said about how to live in the Lord "until we meet again"? I believe that it is crucial to healing from grief to focus our minds, not on terrible images of death, but instead on the human heart's need for God and the reality of our heavenly home.

To help you in this process I am placing here in this chapter more excerpts from the writings of Charles Rich (from "Give me your Heart: Preparing for Eternal Life") for it was precisely the charism of this holy man to invite his friends into deeper contemplation of the supernatural realm. As you read, perhaps insert your own name at the beginning of each passage.

"It is only those who have affectionate natures who are capable of experiencing all the delight divine things have in them. Few know God to be pure Beauty, pure Truth and pure Love. Many know God all right, but they do so in a merely theoretical and abstract way; a way in which it is insufficient for them to make Him the mainstay of their lives...not enough to set their souls afire and to be consumed thereby.

"When we enter a perfume shop we come out with the fragrances that are there and the same thing takes place when we think of all that God has laid up for us after we leave this life.

"By means of sublime dreams God gives us a taste of the joys awaiting us in the life to come.

"What an amazing thing the love of one human being is for another, and what an utter nothing is the earthly love for that human being compared to the one we shall have for him in the life to come? Do we ever think of the kind of love we shall have for each other in the life to come...freed from the limitations which in the present life surround that love?

"Everything on earth is only a symbol and metaphor. We live in a world of signs for what exists in heaven.

"To know what heaven is like, we have to pray for the grace to have some of its quality in ourselves – there is no other way it's joys may be experienced while we are still on earth.... what is heaven but a state of bliss for which no other word can be found? What is heaven but a state of being to which the laws of geography do not apply? Heaven is not something to be understood by our feeble intellect, because the nature of it transcends anything we are able to conceive...the Jews of old referred to heaven as a 'land flowing with milk and honey' into which the mystical Moses that Christ is would one day bring all those who by the lives they led have become worthy of entering into it... (If there were not these riches within us Jesus would not have said) 'The kingdom of heaven is within you.' Heaven is close by, closer than we are to our own selves – its nature and essence constituting the highest region of our being. We do not have to ascend upward; we have but to enter deep within ourselves and we will certainly find it there.

"We would like to know by personal experience what heaven is like, but the best way this can be done is to contemplate all our Lord is both body and soul. Was He not a kind of heaven when He moved among men? ...We shall never be able to get a better idea of what heaven is like than by contemplating all Our Lord is. What is the Sacred Name of Jesus but another word for heaven. By loving Him we get a taste of the joys of heaven.

"Our whole problem in this life is a question of love. As we grow older this love for the right things becomes more purified and refined and this is why interior things are such a joy to the soul – the soul that knows no old age and which is rendered fresher and more vigorous with the passage of time. As we draw closer to our home in Heaven the happier we become and the less distance there is between that in ourselves and that for which we have always longed so much – beatitude.

"The saints in heaven are with each other in a way quite different from the one on earth... you are something more to me than just another human being – you become something I cannot completely fathom, some sweet and wonderful mystery I shall completely understand only after this life is over. We are all mysteries...As the Psalmist says 'I give you thanks that I am fearfully, wonderfully made.' (Psalm 13:14?) ...We are all fearfully, wonderfully made and so we should have this in view all the time we think of ourselves or some other person with whom we are intimately bound up...Friendship provides us with the opportunity of sharing ourselves with someone, first, Christ, and then His members...

"Heaven will consist in the sweetness we will derive from

being close to God and we can get a taste of it on this earth by being close to Him here.

"The sea takes you out of time and helps the soul to think of eternity which the almost limitless stretches of ocean water resemble.

"If we look back at our childhood days we will quickly find traces of the atmosphere of heaven.

"People look forward to a vacation. Why not look forward to heaven. It is a grace for which we must ask.

"My prayer is getting lost in God.

"Though every human being and everything natural are great and good things, they are surpassed infinitely by what is divine and what is supernatural.

"We have been asked not to depend on creatures not because they are not good…everything God has made is good, but because of their limited and circumscribed nature. Creatures are not everywhere available but God is and so when we need a friend most he may for all kinds of legitimate reasons not be around. God alone is always dependable…always around… God has created the good things in this life for our use but for absolute dependence we have to go to Him who is everywhere and always present. We must love our friends, but to depend upon them all the time is not what God wants us to do.

"Christ is joy; He is beauty itself and sublimity and above all, He is the divine delight in which we shall become immersed after we have the grace to enter into another and infinitely more beautiful world than the one in which we now find ourselves; and being what we are, sojourners in a foreign country; we cannot but look forward to this delight as we do in nothing else.

"We shall, throughout eternity, revel in the beauty of Christ's being and we shall there revel in the love in Himself we will then have the grace to have.

"I would like to write a book with the title "Dare to Love,"" because it takes daring of soul to love that which is divine in itself...people are afraid to let go of their hearts with the love they have for God and for each other.

"Christ alone can give us that which will make us happy for all eternity, namely, freedom from the many miseries to which we are now subjected.

"Heaven is the natural home for souls like ours, and it is there our hearts should be centered...not on earth with its imperfect way of experiencing the divine.

"I am anxious to get out of this world so the scope of my activity may increase."

"It is not spiritual exercises that make you holy but the grace. The exercises dispose you for the grace.

"In saying 'Let Him kiss me with the kisses of His mouth' (The Song of Songs), the soul prays to be penetrated by the spirit of Christ and impregnated by His being. The kiss is symbolic of the action of the Holy Spirit which takes place in the substance of the soul: for among the different degrees of union with God we can attain in this life, that denoted by the kiss is the sweetest and most sublime of all. After passing through the different stages of the spiritual life the soul realizes there exists a state higher than all, and it's for this it asks when it says "Let Him kiss me with the kisses of His mouth."

"He mystically is ourselves by being the being of our being and the love of all things lovable.

"Prayer is the longing desire for the divine.

"True prayer is longing for death, the more ardent the longing is, the better we pray.

"'Set my soul free from prison,' the Psalmist prays, 'that I may praise thy name.' We cannot adequately praise God in the present life and so this constitutes a strong motive for wanting to be released from it – we wish to be there where this can be properly done, heaven and there only. To be fully with God we have to die, there being no other way in which can enter into perfect relationship with that which is divine...By allowing us to die, God takes away from us a good that is finite to give us one that is infinite."

"We will have in Christ all created good things, and so nothing will then be wanting to the soul which it now finds so necessary to have.

"There is a phrase in the Sacred Scriptures with a haunting quality about it and it runs like this: "Be prepared O Israel, to meet thy God."

Now by 'Israel' is meant every human being who genuinely loves God and whose main concern in this life is to look forward with joy to being with Him in heaven.

"We are heading for Heaven; earth is departing and the years that pass away are the vehicle that's taking us there...With baited breath we long to be Home with God....We cannot answer a lot of questions this side of the grave, but we will know when we pass the boundary line which separates time from eternity.

"The saints regarded each other with a holy kind of awe, and if we were as holy as they, we would do the same thing."

And here are some of Charles Rich's favorite quotations from the saints:

St. Bernard "We cannot now form an adequate idea of the capacity for love which the soul will have in the next life."

St. Therese "I thought I was going to die and my heart nearly broke with joy."

John of the Cross wrote:

"Creatures are the crumbs fallen from the table of God and which serve to whet the appetite for the divine good and beauty Jesus is...the soul lives where she loves more than in the body she animates; for she does not live in the body, but rather gives life to the body, and lives through love in the object of her love.'"

I would like to add this line here from the poetry of a soon to be canonized saint, John Paul the Great: "When I contain the dual weight of terror and hope and reach depths translucent as sky, then no one will say that I simplify."

For Personal Reflection and Group Sharing:
- Meditate each day on eternal joy with the ones you loved who have left this earth, picturing them waiting for you and yourself, one day, embracing each of them.
- Talk to those who have died, telling them of your sorrows and joys.
- Ask God to teach you how to hold hands with your beloveds in the dark.
- Talk to Jesus all day offering your sorrows in union with His.

Conclusion

"Be still and know that I am God"

(Psalm 46:10)

"Through him you have confidence in God, who raised him from the dead and gave him glory, so that our faith and hope are in God."

(1 Peter 1:21)

On the opening page of Weeping with Jesus, I outlined the theme of this book with these words:

Weep alone – you may drown in grief
Do not weep – you may become hardened
Weep with Jesus – you will have comfort and hope

My hope is that having shared the pain of loss and the insights of those cited in *Weeping with Jesus: the Journey from Grief to Hope* and, especially, the beautiful Scripture and tradition of the Church, you will truly have greater hope for your own pilgrimage. Perhaps you will agree with me that the purpose of God allowing the miseries of death and grief is to gradually wean us from the world and bind us to Him who is "The Way, the Truth and the Life." The only way through grief is Christ. It is His saving truths we need to hang onto in faith; so that we will one day join Him whose Divinity is abundant life. Our home, where we hope to be re-united with our loved ones who have gone before, is not here on earth, but in heaven. Our tears become a river to sail on into the heart of God.

Bibliography

Angela of Foligno: Complete Works, translated with an introduction by Paul Lachance, O.F.M. (New York: Paulist Press, 1993)

St. Augustine, *Confessions,* translated with an introduction by R.S. Pine-Coffin (London: Penguin Books, 1961)

St. Augustine, *City of God*, Vol. 18 Great Books of the Western World (Chicago: Encyclopedia Brittanica, 1952)

Barrack, Martin K. *Eternal Israel*. Unpublished manuscript.

Catechism of the Catholic Church (Libreria Editrice Vaticana, 1994)

Chervin, Martin, *Children of the Breath* - Dialogues of Christ and Satan during the 40 days in the Desert (Oak Lawn, Ill.: CMJ Marian Publishers, 1998)

Chervin, Martin, *Born/Unborn* – a pro-life play about abortion – (Oak Lawn, Ill.: CMJ Marian Publishers)

Myself, Alma Mahler, (a one woman play about Alma and Gustav Mahler) – available from Ronda at rondachervin@gmail.com

Chervin, Ronda. *The Fabric of Our Lives* (Oak Lawn, Ill.: CMJ Marian Publishers, 2000)

Chervin, Ronda. *Help in Time of Need* (Ann Arbor, Michigan: Servant, 2002)

Chervin, Ronda. *Holding Hands with God: Catholic Women Share their Stories of Courage and Hope* (Huntington, Indiana: Our Sunday Visitor, 1997)

Chervin, Ronda. *A Mother's Treasury of Prayers* (Ann Arbor, Michigan: Servant Books, 1994)

Chervin, Ronda. *Quotable Saints* (Ann Arbor: Mich. : Servant, 1992)

Chervin, Ronda. *Seeking Christ in the Crosses and Joys of Aging* (Oak Lawn, Illinois: CMJ Marian Publishers, 2000)

Chervin, Ronda. *Taming the Lion Within: Five Steps from Anger to Peace* (Hayward, California: Café Press, 2003)

Chervin, Ronda. *Treasury of Women Saints* (Ann Arbor: Michigan, Servant Books, 1991)

Chervin, Ronda. *Victory Over Death* (Petersham, Massachusetts, St. Bede's, 1985)

Chervin, Ronda. *A Widow's Walk: Encouragement, Comfort and Wisdom from the Widow-Saints* (Huntington, Indiana: Our Sunday Visitor, 1998)

Dostoevsky, Fyodor, *The Possessed*, trans. Constance Garnet (NY: Macmillan, 1931)

Eltz, Nicky. *Get Us Out of Here!* (The Medjugorje BiH, 2002)

Francis de Sales and Jane de Chantal. *Letters of Spiritual Direction*, translated by Peronne Marie Thibert, V.H.M. (New York: Paulist Press, 1988)

Hardon, Fr. John A.,S.J., *The Treasury of Catholic Wisdom* (San Francisco: Ignatius Press, 1987)

Jorgensen, Johannes. *Saint Bridget of Sweden*, translated by Ingebord Lund (New York: Longmans Green and Co., 1954).

Jürgens, William A. *The Faith of the Early Fathers*, Volume 1 (Collegeville, Minnesota: The Liturgical Press, 1970)

Kreeft, Peter. *Love is Stronger than Death* (San Francisco: Harper, 1987)

Lewis, C.S. *A Grief Observed* (New York, The Seabury Press, 1961)

Lewis, C.S. *The Problem of Pain* (New York: Simon and Schuster, 1976)

Marie of the Incarnation: Selected Writings, edited by Irene Mahoney, O.S.U. (New York: Paulist Press, 1989)

Mazaleski, Leigh T., *When Words Have Wings* (North Carolina, 2001)

Mucha, M. Constance, *Gently Grieving: Taking Care of Yourself and Telling Your Story* (NY Paulist press, 2006)

Olive, Martin-Maria, O. P. *Praxedes: Wife, Mother, Widow and Lay Dominican* (Rockford, Ill.: Tan Books and Publishers, 1987)

Packer, George. *The Assassin's Gate – America in Iraq* (New York: Farrar, Strauss & Giroux, 2005)

Phillipon, M.M., O.P., editor. *Conchita, a Mother's Spiritual Diary*. Translated by Aloysius J. Owens, S.J. Staten Island: Alba House, 1978)

Ratisbonne, Theodore, *Saint Bernard of Clairvaux* (Rockford, Ill.: Tan Books, 1991)

Rich, Charles. *"Give me your Heart" - Preparing for Eternal Life* (unpublished excerpts from the thoughts and writings of Charles Rich by Ronda Chervin – 2006 See www.friendsof-charlesrich.com)

Tyler, Anne. *Digging to America* (N.Y.: Knopf, 2006)

Von Hildebrand, Alice. *By Grief Refined* (Steubenville, Ohio: Franciscan University Press, 1994)

Von Hildebrand, Dietrich. *Jaws of Death: Gate of Heaven* (Manchester, N.H.: Sophia Institute Press, 1991)

Wadham, Juliana. *The Case of Cornelia Connelly* (New York: Pantheon, 1957)

Wurmbrand, Richard. *Sermons in Solitary Confinement* (Diane Books, P. O. Box 2947, Torrance, CA 90509, 1979)

Prayers for the Dead:
Traditional and Contemporary

"How dreadful it would be…if God were indifferent to sin….
to how we used our free will…Does not God's judgment show
forth His infinite love in the ultimate seriousness with which
He regards the depths of our soul?"

(Von Hildebrand, *Jaws of Death: Gate of Heaven*, p. 102)

In certain ways we would prefer to believe that everyone goes
straight to heaven after death. In that case there would be no reason to fear
for ourselves or to pray for those probably in purgatory. But, in fact, we
want our God to be a true Father: just, and merciful, and such a God does
judge us and wants us to pray for ourselves as sinners and also for those
who have left this world, most of them also sinners.

TRADITIONAL PRAYERS

Hail Mary, full of grace The Lord is with you
Blessed are you among women
And blessed is the fruit of your womb, Jesus
Holy Mary, mother of God, pray for us sinners,

now, and at the hour of our death. Amen.

**

At Fatima the visionaries were told to add this prayer at the end of each decade of the rosary: "Oh my Jesus, forgive us our sins, save us from the fires of hell, lead all souls to heaven, especially those in most need of your mercy."

This prayer was allegedly revealed to St. Gertrude the Great by Our Lord, and he promised to release 1,000 souls from Purgatory when it is recited with love and devotion!

> Eternal Father, I offer You the Most Precious Blood of Thy Divine Son, Jesus, in union with all the Masses being said throughout the world today for all the Holy Souls in Purgatory, for sinners everywhere, those in the Universal Church, in my home and within my family. Amen.

**

Jesus, Mary, Joseph, I love you, save souls!

**

From the Office for the Dead - Morning Prayer

God of the living and the dead, you raised Jesus from the dead; raise up those who have died and grant that we may share eternal glory with them.

**

Lord God,
You are the glory of believers and the life of the just.
Your Son redeemed us

by dying and rising to life again.
Our brother (sister)
was faithful and believed in our own resurrection.
Give to him (her) the joy and blessings of the life to come.

**

Father,
Source of forgiveness and salvation for all mankind,
hear our prayer.
By the prayers of the ever-virgin Mary, may our friends,
relatives, and benefactors who have gone from this world come
to share eternal happiness with all your saints.

**

From the Roman Missal:
"Father, accept this offering from your whole family.
Grant us your peace in this life, save us from final damnation,
and count us among those you have chosen."

**

"You opened Paradise to the thief who believed in you, do not close
the gates of heaven to the faithful departed."
(Liturgy of the Hours, Week III, Friday Evening Prayer Intercessions)

**

Stations of the Cross – Pray the Stations in the Church or elsewhere
using a booklet, offering your prayers for your beloved dead person you
believe to be in purgatory.

CONTEMPORARY

Chaplet of Mercy

This prayer given to St. Faustina in the first half of the 20th century has become a favorite for praying for the dead as well as the living.

On the large Our Father beads:

Eternal Father,
we offer you
the Body and Blood, Soul and Divinity,
of Your dearly beloved Son, Our Lord, Jesus Christ,
in atonement for our sins and those of the whole world.

And on the little decades of beads: For the sake of His sorrowful passion, have mercy on us and on the whole world. At the end, say 3 x.

Holy God, Holy Mighty One, Holy Immortal One, have mercy on us and on the whole world.

Specific Prayer to Mary Exalted Widow

O Mary, conceived without original sin, I pray…for the gift of spiritual peace….
You whose heart was pierced by a sword,
As prophesied by Simon at the presentation
Of Jesus in the Temple,
To whom was prophesied by the widow Anna,
Who suffered the death of your holy spouse, Joseph,
You who stood at the foot of the cross,
Contemplating the death of your Son
For sinners, and accepted the plan of the Father,
I pray that you would intercede for me,
That with your example of supreme faith,
I would accept the will of the Lord,

in the hope of receiving the grace to be reunited with everyone
in his holy kingdom.

Amen.

**

Prayer for a Miscarried or Still Born Baby

Flown like a bird into the arms of God?

Too good for his (her) feet to touch the ground?

But I wanted that baby so much, Lord!

Did you think I was not worthy to mother that baby?

Or was it your way to prevent this baby

from suffering in this world?

I feel very empty, Jesus.

Help me to accept your permissive will.

Help me to have courage to try again.

Help me to rejoice that this baby does exist and will live

for all eternity and that one day I will see my baby as a grown person

when my time on earth is over.

I offer you the pain in my heart that you may use it just as you

wish for your glory and honor, Amen

> Grace Geist, in *A Mother's Treasury of Prayers*, edited by
> Ronda Chervin (Ann Arbor, Michigan: Servant Books,
> 1994) p. 64

**

Prayer for an Aborted Baby

I come to you, my Jesus stricken with remorse

about the baby

whose face I never saw.

I didn't really believe in your love when I did it.

I just knew I couldn't handle it.

121

Couldn't handle telling my parents,
my boyfriend's rejection
But now that I am a woman who knows who you are
I wonder about that aborted baby.
Where is he or she?
I feel your arms around me.
I see you pointing to your mother and showing me my babe
lying in her lap with her tears
flowing like baptismal water.
Can you show me that my baby is safe
in spite of my dread deed?
Please help me to forgive myself,
and help my baby to forgive me.
You told us that
"Love covers a multitude of sins."
May your love cover my sins.
If there is a way
I can help other women who seek abortion
as what seems to them to be their only solution, show me how.

(Based on words of Janet Krupnick from
A Mother's Treasury of Prayers, p. 66-67)

**

Prayer for a Teen who Died
It's over.
Nothing I can do.
My dead child,
lying in the cold morgue.
I prayed that you would resurrect (name)
just as you raised Lazarus,

but you didn't answer me.
I want to be able to forgive all those people
who were involved in this death; who caused it,
or who could have prevented it, but I am having trouble
with my angry feelings.
Give me the grace to say as you did, my Jesus,
'Father, forgive them, they know not what they do.'
Sometimes I even feel angry with you
when I think that you could have changed everything
so that my child would not have died.
Yet I realize
that only you can save my child in eternity,
only you can bring us back together in the joy of heaven.
Like Mary,
I would hold my child in my lap.
But even this has not been granted me.
Mary, teach me how to hold my dead child in my heart;
to give him (her) to you to hold
until we are all together again.

      Diana De Sola (*A Mother's Treasury of Prayers*, p. 160-161)

www.ingramcontent.com/pod-product-compliance
Lightning Source LLC
Chambersburg PA
CBHW022013090426

42741CB00007B/1022